Snatched

ELIZABETH HARPER

My True Story of Survival

WITH VERONICA CLARK

Snatched

Trapped by a woman
to be sold to men

Certain details in this story, including names, places and dates,
have been changed to protect the identities
of certain individuals.

HarperElement
An imprint of HarperCollins*Publishers*
1 London Bridge Street
London SE1 9GF

www.harpercollins.co.uk

HarperCollins*Publishers*
1st Floor, Watermarque Building, Ringsend Road
Dublin 4, Ireland

First published by HarperElement 2022

1 3 5 7 9 10 8 6 4 2

A catalogue record of this book is
available from the British Library

ISBN 978-0-00-850321-5

Printed and bound in the UK using 100%
renewable electricity at CPI Group (UK) Ltd

To my family and Risky Business project
for always being there

'Rotherham wasn't a mistake; it was a conspiracy. Children were fed to the wolves while the perpetrators were allowed to roam free.'

ELIZABETH HARPER, AUGUST 2021

CHAPTER ONE

THE BUS STOP

It was freezing cold, but my legs burned as I trudged along the street, desperate to try to waste the rest of the day. Countless windows stared down at me and I felt like a specimen underneath the intense lens of a microscope. The street was far too public; there was a risk of being spotted – I had to hide. I'd been walking for most of the day and my body felt numbed by the cold air. Mum had been on the wrong shift that day, so my stint indoors had been temporarily scuppered. I strolled a little further along before slipping sideways, diverting away from the main road, into a maze of smaller cut-through paths that linked the estate. The narrow flagstone paths spread like feathery veins, which made it much easier to blend in. To the outside world, I was just another girl making her way home early from school. School. I hated it with a passion. My life had been almost unbearable since I'd started at the new secondary. I'd always been a real bookworm – naturally academic – which had made me unpopular in class; that, and the fact that I wanted to become a teacher. Once my passion for books became general knowledge, I became a prime target for bullies. I decided that the easiest way to swerve them would be to avoid school and vanish from lessons altogether. My first escape had been easy, thanks to a torn piece of fencing that I'd discovered in the bottom right-hand corner of the playing field. The broken fence had been my get-out-of-jail-free card; out of sight, out of mind. It had been so easy that soon I began to bunk off every day, and I'd got away with it for six long weeks until parents' evening. I refused to go to school that night, but Mum and Dad went and, as soon as they came in through the door, they demanded answers.

'Why the hell haven't you been going to school?' Mum asked.

She stood there, annoyed and hovering over me, waiting for an answer. Dad flopped down in an armchair opposite. The disappointment on his face was unbearable. I wasn't sure what to do. I refused to say I'd been bullied because I knew it would only make things ten times worse, so instead I shrugged my shoulders with typical teenage nonchalance. But my indifference seemed to enrage Mum more.

'Well,' she huffed, clearly exasperated, 'if you can't be trusted to go there then we're going to have to start taking you ourselves.'

The thought of being dropped off at school by my parents left me mortified. If anything, I knew it would only give the bullies more ammunition to fire back. However, I had no plans to stay in school, so I knew that it really wouldn't make much difference. Instead, I would go along to the morning register, then leave through the broken fence. The school was on my case, of course. Even though I was thirteen and pretty clever, my constant absence affected my schoolwork. The next time I was confronted, I had no other option than to come clean, especially as I'd been summoned to the headmaster's office, along with my parents.

'It's these three girls … they're really nasty to me,' I began to explain, my legs swinging below me and the chair. The blunt edge of the cheap grey plastic seat bit against the backs of my knees.

The headmaster sighed as though he'd heard it all before. He knew I'd already missed far too much school-work to try to catch up, and besides, I'd continue to bolt if he forced me to go back. Instead, he leaned back in his chair and considered my options. Finally, he sat forward and rested both his elbows on his mahogany desk.

'It's imperative that Elizabeth keeps up with her maths, English and science …' he explained as Mum and Dad nodded along in agreement. 'So, I suggest we give her a timetable that works around these subjects. If Elizabeth comes into school to complete these lessons – say, one lesson a day – then I would allow her to return home afterwards.'

My folks didn't seem exactly thrilled with his solution, but if it meant the difference between getting an education or not, they had no choice.

'Okay,' Mum agreed.

Initially, I had stuck to the headmaster's plan, but my heart wasn't really in it, and it wasn't very long before I slipped back into my old ways. I'd already had a taste of freedom and now I craved it – my own space to do whatever I wanted. I couldn't return to school, not now, not ever.

My behaviour continued unchanged and unchallenged until a year later. With a shocking attendance record behind me, I turned fifteen. By this time, I was adept at prowling the streets to kill time. No one seemed to care. My parents, who had always taken my education seriously, weren't aware that I was still bunking off, and my teachers' indifference made me despise school even more. The comprehensive school itself was lax and the teachers adopted a very laid-back approach when dealing with students. They certainly weren't going to miss me. In fact, one less child to teach would have been considered a bit of a blessing.

It's a total waste of time. What do I need maths or science for? I thought as I took the long way home along my usual street of choice.

I mulled it over, trying to justify it to myself, but I was a typical teenager, and right then it felt like me against the rest of the world.

Mum and Dad worked at a local supermarket, so they would leave at the same time. However, some days their shift patterns would change and give me a small window of opportunity – the chance to nip home late morning or early afternoon. Whenever this happened, I would sit and watch TV for a few hours, sneak back out and retrace my route before pretending to return to our semi-detached council house for the very first time. However, their shifts weren't set in stone and often differed week to week, leaving my days unpredictable. Soon, I seemed to be dodging everyone: the bullies, my parents and the teachers. My truancy meant that I was always alone and, as a result, I felt adrift. I didn't realise it then, but this made me extremely vulnerable.

One day in autumn 2003, I'd been through the usual motions of trying to kill time and was walking along a small pathway – one I knew like the back of my hand –

that eventually re-joined the main road. There was a bus stop up ahead and a small queue of people standing by it. My eyes quickly scanned the blur of faces, but no one looked remotely familiar. Still, I bowed my head. As I passed the queue, I felt a pair of eyes following me. A flash of white cloth billowed out like a freshly laundered sheet on a washing line, catching in my peripheral vision. I noticed it but I didn't turn around. Instead, I carried on walking, but someone was watching me, I could just sense it. Tilting my face upwards, I scoured the dozens of windows that overlooked me. I'd expected to see someone standing there, monitoring me, but all the windows were empty. Baffled, I shook the thought from my head and pressed further on along the road.

A few days later, I retraced my way along the same route through the estate. My steps weaved in and out from the main road like a zig-zag stitch, trying to avoid detection. The familiar bus stop was up ahead on the right at the top of a slight hill. There were a few people waiting for the bus, including a woman wearing a white hijab. The wind blew and caught against it and the hijab billowed out like a small, white sail. I didn't tend to see many people wearing traditional Pakistani clothing, so I found the woman fascinating. As I drew near, I averted my eyes and tried to focus on the chewing-gum-splattered pavement. I counted the grey-white misshapen splodges on the tarmac for something to do.

Five ... six ... seven ...

As I approached, I momentarily glanced up and the woman in the hijab did something quite unexpected: her face broke into a large, warm smile, as though she recognised me. Her reaction left me completely stumped.

Do I know her? I wondered, trying not to look but now unable to stop myself. I decided that I didn't.

But why is she still staring?

A sudden thought flashed across my mind.

Does she know Mum or Dad?

I couldn't be sure, so I glanced back at her. The woman's eyes locked with mine; her gaze was so intense that it felt rude to look away.

'Hello,' she said, still smiling.

'Hi,' I mumbled, half smiling back at her.

The whole encounter felt awkward, but when my eyes looked back at her a few seconds later I noticed that she was laughing.

Is she laughing at me? I thought, feeling slightly annoyed.

The woman was rather large – around a size 18 or 20 – and so quite conspicuous, even in a crowd. Once I had noticed her, I was intrigued.

Maybe we've passed each other in the street before.

Although I very much doubted that because I was certain I would've remembered. I had grown up and lived in Rotherham, South Yorkshire, with my parents and younger sister, Claire. She was three years younger than me and we got on well. The council estate that I lived on was populated by predominantly white, working-class families, so it was unusual to see a woman dressed like that around there. I couldn't work out how or where I knew her from, and I couldn't explain it but upon seeing her, an uneasy feeling flooded through me. The hairs on the back of my neck stood on end and prickled against my skin. The strange woman was acting as though she knew me, but she also seemed a little overfamiliar.

My stomach growled loudly, interrupting my thoughts and reminding me that I hadn't eaten since breakfast. I was absolutely starving! I inched up the sleeve of my jumper so that I could check the time. I groaned.

Still another hour to kill!

My eyes rolled in annoyance. The minutes seemed to drag by, and I found myself walking in circles until eventually it was time to go home. As soon as I bounded in through the back door I headed straight for the fridge. My hands were still searching for something quick to eat when Mum walked into the kitchen.

'Don't go stuffing yourself; you'll ruin your appetite,' she said, as she went over to the worktop and began to peel some potatoes. The sharp knife sliced the skins quickly, removing them within seconds. Satisfied, she placed the last peeled spud in the colander and turned to face me.

'Have you got any homework?'

But I wasn't really listening. I had sat down at the kitchen table and was absentmindedly flicking through a TV listings magazine. I turned the page with one hand and buried the other inside a packet of crisps.

'Hmm?' I mumbled.

'Homework?' Mum repeated.

I shook my head.

'No, not tonight.'

She nodded, satisfied by my answer.

The school doesn't give a shit – they obviously haven't told her I've haven't even been there.

'Make yourself useful and set the table, will you?' she said, calling over her shoulder.

I groaned but stood up and did as she said; I couldn't be bothered to argue. Not tonight.

A few days later, I was walking along the street when I stopped to check the time.

Half past two.

I had recently fallen into a pattern of treading the same route almost every day, more through familiarity than anything else. I knew exactly how long each street, each avenue and each estate would take me to walk. Eventually, I re-joined the main road with the familiar bus stop just up ahead. Once again, I noticed the strange woman – the one who had spoken to me. My stomach clenched with anxiety. She was wearing the same patterned tunic, and her black leggings strained at the seams as though fighting to keep her legs hidden inside. The hijab draped down both sides of her face and over her shoulders, making her look a little like a nun, its white fabric reflected in the weak spring sunshine. As I climbed the small hill, I realised that she was doing it again – she was staring at me. By size alone, I found her quite intimidating.

'Hello,' she said, her face breaking into a wide smile.

'Hi,' I replied, only this time I didn't look away. I was trying to figure out where I knew her from.

'You seem a bit lost,' she remarked as her forehead creased and furrowed with worry. 'Are you lost?'

She took a step forward and was now standing directly in front of me, blocking my path. The whole situation felt a little odd, as though she wanted to stop and chat.

Maybe she's lonely.

Even though she was the only person at the bus stop, the pavement was narrow, so it was impossible to try to push past. For now, I was trapped; as I glanced up, I realised that she was still waiting for an answer.

'You seem a little lost ...' she repeated in case I hadn't heard the first time.

'No, I'm fine. I'm just on my way home ...' I insisted. I lifted a hand and gestured off into the middle-distance.

However, the woman didn't seem convinced.

'Well, you don't look it; in fact, you look really miserable.'

My stomach clenched.

Who is she? Is she something to do with the school? Is she going to report me?

I was just wondering how to respond when she added: 'What is it? Boy trouble?'

My face burned as my face blushed; I didn't even have a boyfriend!

'Ahh, is that it? Have I guessed correctly? Is it a boy?' she said, as though teasing me.

I shook my head furiously.

'No.'

Lifting her right hand, the woman pushed and shrugged the hijab away from her left shoulder.

'Okay ... well, if it's not boy trouble then it must be school,' she said, guessing correctly.

My face flushed once more as heat rose in my cheeks.

'I knew it!'

The stranger was staring at me so intently that I was now feeling a bit uncomfortable. She seemed to sense it and started to back away.

'Sorry ... I don't mean to pry. It's just that I've got a daughter, Donna. She's a similar age to you, and she doesn't like school very much either. To be honest, she doesn't go because she has so many problems when she ...'

The woman stopped as though she'd already said too much, but by now I was all ears. She spotted this and began to elaborate.

'I said to her, "Donna, if it makes you that unhappy then you don't have to go. I mean, what's the point? Why make yourself unhappy?"'

I found myself nodding along as she continued.

'… I mean, she's my daughter and I want her to be happy, but I don't want her wasting her life at school, doing lessons and being with kids who make her miserable. I mean, what's the point?'

By now I was utterly captivated.

Why isn't my mum more like her? I thought bitterly. *Why do I have to go to school when it makes me so unhappy?*

There was a moment's silence as the woman waited for a reply, and that's when I realised she had asked me a question.

'Sorry?'

'I said, do you know what I mean? Anyway, listen to me, rattling on. You must think I'm an old …'

'Yeah, I mean, no! I hate school; it's a total waste of time. That's why I don't go.'

The woman paused and looked me up and down as though taking me all in.

'You sound just like my Donna,' she added.

She pulled a cigarette out from a pocket in her tunic and began to light it. The embers burned brightly as the flame took hold and she blew some grey smoke out from the corner of her mouth.

'Sorry, where are my manners? Do you want one?' she asked, holding the open packet of cigarettes towards me.

I was so shocked that I shook my head; I'd never smoked before in my life.

'Suit yourself,' she said, flipping the lid of the packet shut. 'I'll tell you what, though, you should meet my daughter; you should meet Donna. You two would get on like a house on fire!'

With the cigarette wedged between two fingers, she pointed it away from her as her eyes scanned mine.

'Don't tell Donna I said this, but she could really do with a friend like you.'

An unexpected smile spread across my face. I couldn't help myself.

Donna sounds just like me!

'Oh, but then I bet you've got loads of friends. You probably don't need another one …' she said, immediately dismissing the idea.

'No … that'd be great!' I replied a little too quickly. 'I mean … I'd really like to meet her.'

'Okay, we'll organise something then.'

This had suddenly turned into a great day. Soon, I couldn't wipe the smile from my face; I was just so delighted that I was going to meet someone else – a girl my age – who knew exactly what it felt like to be me.

'I'd really like that.'

Suddenly the conversation reached a natural end. Unsure what to do, I turned as though to leave.

'Oh, I almost forgot to ask,' the woman said, taking a drag of her fag. 'What's your name?'

'Elizabeth. It's El … El Harper.'

She threw the half-smoked cigarette to the floor and crushed it out with the sole of her shoe.

'Well, it's nice to meet you, El. I'm Shafina, by the way, and I could meet you here tomorrow – around the same time?'

I nodded gratefully.

'... and I'll bring Donna with me.'

I was thrilled that I'd finally have the chance to make a new friend; not only a friend, but someone just like me. I was certain that Donna wouldn't judge me like the other girls at school did, because she was in the exact same situation.

The following day, I repeatedly checked my watch, waiting and praying for half past two to arrive so that I could meet Shafina and her daughter, Donna.

What if they're not there? What if it's a trick?

I shook my head.

Why would a grown woman want to trick me?

Sure enough, as soon as I turned the corner I spotted Shafina, although she seemed to see me before I'd seen her. As she lifted her hand to wave, I noticed she was wearing a black hijab instead of her usual white one. There was a young girl, who I presumed must be Donna, standing next to her. Unlike Shafina, Donna was wearing plain jeans and a jumper – westernised clothes. Excitement rose inside me and my footsteps seemed to quicken. But as I grew closer, I realised that Donna didn't look half as excited to see me as I did her. In fact, judging from the scowl on her face, she didn't seem very friendly at all.

'Hi, El, this is Donna. Say hello,' Shafina said, giving her daughter a gentle nudge against the small of her back.

'All right?' Donna mumbled, looking off to the side as though she hated every second of being there.

'Yeah, you?'

The young girl looked me up and down and I suddenly felt extremely conscious of my horrible black shoes and tight school trousers. I felt a little stupid and guessed that I probably looked so to someone as cool as Donna. It was clear this girl wasn't the same age as me. In fact, she looked a few years older. There was a moment's silence as Donna chewed some gum and clacked it sharply inside her mouth. It was obvious from her body language – the sneer on her face and her arms folded tightly across her chest – that I wasn't welcome. Donna didn't want to be my friend; in fact, she could barely even look at me.

'Donna, stop it. Now,' Shafina snapped.

She put her hand deep inside her tunic pocket and felt around inside it. The shiny synthetic fabric shone as it clung to her bloated stomach, emphasising it. 'I've got it here somewhere. Hang on … ah, here it is!' she said, pulling out a scrap of paper. 'Here,' she said, pressing it into my palm. 'This is our address. Come round any time you like; you're always welcome, isn't she, Donna?'

The teenager shrugged as though she didn't care either way.

No wonder she doesn't have friends, I decided.

'Thanks,' I said, folding the scrap of paper tightly inside my hand. 'And I will. I'll come and see you soon.'

'You do that. Oh, look, the bus is coming,' said Shafina, looking behind me and over my shoulder.

She took a step forward and held out her hand as the bus pulled up alongside the kerb. The doors hissed loudly as they both folded and opened. Shafina raised a foot, grabbed a side pole and climbed onboard.

'Look after yourself, El,' she said, calling back to me.

'You too!' I replied happily.

'And we'll see you soon!'

Donna pushed past us both without a word, but Shafina hadn't finished.

'We're not far from here. Our flat is only round the corner!'

The bus doors hissed once more and snapped closed as it pulled away. As she passed, Shafina smiled and waved at me through the window. I watched as she then lurched forward, grabbing a pole as she tried to get to her seat. I couldn't see Donna, but I could just imagine her scowling and telling Shafina that she didn't want to be mates with me. Although she hadn't been friendly, I was certain that once she'd given me a chance, Donna and I would get on just fine. After all, she was Shafina's daughter, and Shafina was one of the kindest people I'd ever met.

CHAPTER TWO

THE FLAT

Shafina's place was situated on the ground floor of a nondescript brown brick building. It had three levels that contained only flats. The windows were small and boxy, and the property had a bit of a pokey feel about it, even from the outside. The front and only door was at the bottom of four concrete steps, with a white metal handrail leading down to it. There was a sad strip of grass at both the front and back, but neither patch had been fenced off so it couldn't quite be classed as a garden, communal or otherwise; only a walk-through. I stood there for a moment at the bottom of the steps and faced the black uPVC door. The area was covered by a small lean-to roof to keep the rain off. It was 9 a.m. when I lifted my hand and held it in mid-air, wondering whether to knock and, if they answered, what to say.

What if Donna answers?

My stomach flipped with nerves as I remembered Shafina's daughter. She hadn't exactly been overly friendly at the bus stop, so what would she be like if I knocked at her door?

It had been a week since Shafina had handed me her address. My fingers searched for the folded-up scrap of paper buried deep inside my pocket as though looking for some reassurance. I'd been toying with the idea of calling at the flat for days, but I had lost my nerve until now.

Maybe Shafina just felt sorry for me? Maybe she was trying to be nice but didn't think that I would actually take her up on her offer ...

Doubts began to set in and I almost walked away, but something kept me there, standing at the door. Maybe it was because I felt so lonely and was in such desperate need of a friend – any friend – even Donna.

Taking a deep breath for courage, I lifted the gold door knocker and tapped it lightly against the door before I changed my mind.

TAP. TAP. TAP.

For a split second I almost lost my nerve again. I glanced over to my left at a waist-high brick wall that seemed to be more decorative than functional. Above it, there was a small frosted window, which I guessed must be the bathroom. To the right of me there was a much larger window. However, I couldn't see inside because there was a pair of net curtains hanging in the window.

Shafina's flat was only streets from my school, so I knew the estate quite well and I was conscious that I might be spotted. I decided that if there was no answer in the next few minutes I would –

'Hi, El. Come in, come in,' Shafina smiled.

She waved her hand and beckoned me inside. As she did, a deep band of silver bangles jangled loudly together around her fleshy wrist.

'Hi,' I smiled, taking a nervous step inside.

The first thing that hit me was the smell – a heady mixture of cigarettes, stale air, bad breath and body odour. The flat also smelled of ground-in dirt and unwiped surfaces. Although it was morning, the curtains were drawn and the main light in the hallway switched on. The place felt both squalid and unloved.

'Donna … Donna …' Shafina said, tilting her head to one side. Her eyes didn't leave me, not even for a second. She hollered along the hallway to her daughter, her voice harsh and demanding. 'Get out here now! We have company.'

I suddenly felt really awkward, standing there inside her grimy, half-lit flat. I didn't really know Shafina or her daughter. Shafina turned away and told me to follow her, which I did. Curiosity got the better of me and I stole a quick glance inside each room as we passed. On my left was the bathroom, just as I'd suspected when I'd been standing outside. The kitchen looked sparse and as grubby as the rest of the flat. There was another room off the hallway, which I guessed must be a bedroom, but the door was closed so I couldn't see inside. Then we turned a sharp right and I found myself standing in the main living room with Donna directly in front of me, engrossed in her mobile phone.

Only one bedroom? I wonder where Donna sleeps. Do they share?

I couldn't imagine having to share a bedroom with Mum.

'Look, Donna. It's El,' Shafina said, announcing my arrival to her unimpressed teenage daughter.

Donna barely even glanced up. When she finally did, she only half nodded in recognition before turning her attention back to her mobile phone.

'Listen, I'll go and get El a drink and you two can get to know each other.'

With that, Shafina disappeared, leaving me alone with a surly-looking Donna. The living room was as dark as the rest of the flat. The only source of light was a small side lamp covered by a battered, faded green lampshade. Like the kitchen, the living room seemed pretty sparse apart from two sofas and a coffee table, which took centre stage. The table was covered in a dusting of grey ash and discarded, half-opened cigarette packets, chipped mugs and abandoned glasses that were half-full of liquid. I flinched as I noticed that one glass and two of the mugs had a greenish-grey mould growing inside them.

Donna had flopped down onto one of the sofas and was still scrolling through her phone. The sofas were scuffed and threadbare, as though they had seen better days. A pair of grubby net curtains hung limply against the window. As I looked around, something odd struck me – there was hardly any furniture. The flat contained very little, which made it look and feel as though they didn't plan on hanging around for very long.

It's a bit of a doss house, I decided, feeling grateful that I lived with my parents in a cosy, well-kept home.

With Shafina in the kitchen pouring us a drink, I sat down next to Donna and desperately tried to think of something interesting to say – anything to break the tension between us. I was still thinking when Donna broke the silence first.

'You wear make-up?' she asked, as she scrutinised my bare face.

I nodded, although it was a lie because I didn't wear make-up and never had. In fact, I not only looked but acted far younger than my fifteen years.

'Yeah,' I said, waving at my bare face. 'I mean, I've not got any make-up on today, but I normally do.'

Donna smiled for the first time and sat upright in her seat.

'You want to put some on?'

A grateful warmth flooded through me because I was just so relieved that we were finally becoming friends.

'Yeah, that'd be great!'

She unzipped her make-up bag and pulled out some orangey-brown foundation that was far too tanned for her pale complexion. It was so bad that as soon as I saw it I flinched.

God, I hope she's not going to put that on me!

I didn't voice this worry out loud because at least she was trying to be friendly.

Once she'd smeared the orange foundation all over her face, she pulled out a small tub of chalky white eyeshadow. I gulped; it was absolutely horrible.

'Borrow what you need,' she offered, but because I didn't wear make-up, I didn't have a clue how to apply it.

I decided to follow her lead. I had to show willing, especially if we were going to be friends. Squeezing the tube, I blobbed some of the orange foundation onto my fingertip.

'Oh, and here's some mascara and an eyeliner,' she said, passing it over to me, 'but it needs sharpening. I think there's a sharpener in there,' she added, pointing down at her make-up bag.

I began rooting for the sharpener, so delighted that I was finally part of something – part of Shafina's family, as strange as it was. Anything had to be better than wandering the streets alone. Anything.

Suddenly, a huge figure appeared in the doorway, filling it.

Shafina.

'Ah, you're making friends. Good … good!'

Donna glanced over at her mother with an odd expression on her face that I couldn't quite read.

Maybe that's why she doesn't have any friends. Maybe she finds it difficult to mix.

I had questions. There was obviously a strange atmosphere between Shafina and her daughter and I couldn't figure out why. However, I didn't voice my concerns because I didn't want to rock the boat or upset my new friends; instead, I pushed away any doubts.

'Here,' Shafina said, stepping from the doorway to hand me a drink; it was a glass of cola.

'Thanks.'

The room felt warm because the only window was closed and covered with the dingy net curtain. I gulped at my drink thirstily, and it was immediately obvious that the liquid definitely wasn't cola. Instead of sweet sugar, the drink burned the inside of my mouth and throat, causing me to choke, splutter and then cough. Flushing with embarrassment, I covered my mouth with my hand and desperately tried to clear my airways so I could breathe. I felt such a fool.

Why did I have to gulp it down? I've just made a right show of myself.

However, try as I might, I just couldn't stop spluttering. I put my glass on the coffee table, separating all the abandoned glasses and coffee mugs. The glass pushed a clear snail-trail through the cigarette ash as it slid against the wood.

'What's wrong? It hasn't got bones in it!' Shafina joked as she exploded with laughter.

Feeling humiliated, my eyes darted over towards Donna, who I could tell was trying her best not to laugh.

'You drink Bacardi, don't you?' Shafina asked.

Bacardi – that's what it was. I was fifteen, but, despite bunking off school, I was still very young and naive for my age. While other girls at my school were into rap, I loved the Spice Girls. My favourite was Mel C because she was sporty and she had real attitude.

'Yeah, of course I do,' I replied defensively. My cheeks flushed even more with the lie.

Inwardly I cursed because I didn't want to look stupid in front of my new friends.

'So,' I said, leaving my glass on the coffee table, 'what kind of music do you like?'

Donna had moved from the sofa to the floor, but before she'd had the chance to answer, Shafina answered for her.

'Christina Aguilera, don't you, Donna? She absolutely loves her.'

Shafina's eyes glinted with mischief as I turned to Donna. It seemed to fit. Loads of girls my age liked Christina Aguilera. Although something about this girl told me that she didn't. It could have been the slight eye roll and sigh she gave at the mention of the singer's name. I couldn't be sure, and I doubted that I'd actually seen it for a second, but she had definitely just pulled a face.

'I like the Spice Girls, particularly Mel C. She's not like the others, she's a tomboy …' I garbled, filling the awkward silence.

Shafina held up her hand, cutting me short before she quickly changed the subject.

'In fact,' she said, waltzing dramatically across the room, 'let's put some Christina Aguilera on right now.'

She leaned forward towards a small, black portable CD player perched on top of a side table and pressed a chubby thumb against the play button. Within seconds the whole room filled with Christina Aguilera's distinctive sound. Shafina turned the volume up to full, so the singer's powerful voice soared against the low ceiling before bouncing back down again. As the intro to 'Beautiful' tore from the tinny speakers, an instant tension filled the room. I glanced over at Donna and noticed that she physically flinched as soon as the song started. I wondered how often Shafina played this song. The teenager sat up on her heels as though she was about to say something but then seemed to think better of it.

Shafina began to sing the lyrics to Christina Aguilera's song 'Beautiful', looking at me while stroking her hand along the back of the sofa opposite.

A shudder ran through me; I couldn't explain it, but something was wrong. The atmosphere felt odd, like a misplaced foot at a dance. There was definitely something up with Donna. Before the song, she had started to apply some mascara in the mirror; now it had begun, she stood up and left the room.

Have I said something wrong? Has Shafina?

I wasn't sure what it was, but I hoped it had nothing to do with me. After all, I'd hardly said a word.

No, this is definitely something between Donna, Shafina and the music.

It felt strange, sitting there in the middle of an argument that I had absolutely nothing to do with. Donna already had a bit of an attitude, but this was something else. You could cut the atmosphere between the two of them with a knife. Feeling out of my depth and unsure quite what to do, I sat back on the sofa and sipped at my rum and Coke. The amber liquid seemed to warm me from the inside as it slipped down my throat. Soon, the alcohol relaxed my body, but it also left me feeling a little light-headed as the music washed over me.

The song finished and I wondered what Shafina would play next. She ran over to the CD player and I watched in disbelief as she pressed repeat and the song played over and over again. In fact, she played it so much over the hours that followed that I decided I wouldn't care if I never heard it again.

Poor Donna. No wonder she left the room.

Eventually it was time to leave for home. I glanced over at Shafina, who seemed lost in her own world, still singing along to the music. Furtively, I glimpsed down at the clock on my Nokia mobile. I didn't want to appear rude, checking the time in front of her, but it was three o'clock, and my 'English lesson' had supposedly finished – it was time to go. I stumbled slightly as I rose to my feet. My lack of balance took me by surprise because I'd felt okay when I'd been sitting down. I swayed slightly but managed to regain my balance just as Donna stepped back into the room. I was worried that she would think I was leaving because of her – she was already hard enough to try to win over.

'I'm just, er, I've gotta go,' I mumbled. 'It's Mum, she'll be expecting me.'

The song stopped and Shafina, who had slumped onto the sofa, half opened her eyes, waking from whatever trance she'd been in. She glanced around the room, her dark eyes darting from one spot to another, as though she was seeing it for the very first time.

'El's leaving,' Donna said in a loud voice, trying to prompt her.

Shafina struggled to get up from the sofa. It took a few attempts and a little bit of grunting, but when she finally did she adjusted the black hijab over both shoulders and smoothed down the front of her tunic over her belly.

'It's been so lovely to see you, El. Hasn't it, Donna?'

I couldn't explain it, but her voice sounded forced and insincere as she looked to Donna as though seeking confirmation.

'Yeah.' The young girl shrugged.

'Right then,' I said. I was still feeling a little unsteady as my feet stumbled against the worn, brown living-room carpet. 'I'll be off.'

I drained the rest of my drink in one mouthful and balanced the glass on a corner of the table. With my head still feeling dizzy and my stomach a little woozy, I grabbed the side of the sofa to try to steady myself.

'Whoa, careful, El!' Shafina laughed.

I ignored her and stumbled towards the front door, past a large mirror hanging in the hallway. I was shocked as I caught a glimpse of myself, with my red face and dishevelled hair.

Drunk. You are drunk, a voice inside me said.

Suddenly, the hallway wall seemed to rush at speed towards me before pulling away again.

Am I drunk?

I'd never been drunk before so I didn't know what it felt like. If this was what it was then I decided that I liked it!

'Take care,' Shafina said, opening the front door for me as I staggered through it.

A sudden blast of cool air brushed against my face, hands and body, waking me up. I inhaled a greedy lungful to try to sober up before making my way home.

'Don't forget to come back and see us soon, El!' Shafina called after me. 'Promise?'

I turned and smiled.

'Promise.'

My eyes searched for Donna. I expected her to be standing by her mother's side, but instead she was at the back of the hallway, her arms folded angrily across her pinched little chest, her face cold and unsmiling.

CHAPTER THREE

DONNA

The following morning, I was due in school for a maths lesson but I didn't go. Instead, I headed straight for Shafina's flat.

'El!' she said, throwing her hands up in the air in surprise. 'It's so good to see you.'

Shafina's hand grabbed the top of my arm as she pulled me inside. Although she led me down the hallway, this time I knew exactly where to go.

'Hi, Donna.' I smiled when I saw her, although she didn't return my greeting.

Shafina sidled up against me and began to whisper something in my ear.

'Just ignore her; she's in a bit of a mood today.'

A mood? How would I be able to tell?

'There's nothing wrong with me,' the young girl said, spitting each word out with venom. 'It's you. It's … it's this … isn't it?' she said, waving a hand around the living room.

I glanced around. Donna was right – the place was a mess. The ashtray looked as though it hadn't been emptied for weeks and the grubby nets didn't look as though they'd ever been washed. The flat was a dump.

'Well, you know what you can do if you don't like it,' Shafina retorted.

I looked between them both, not knowing what I'd just walked in on. Whatever the argument had been yesterday, it clearly hadn't gone away.

Shafina seemed to sense my discomfort.

'Drink and a bit of toast?' she offered.

It was only half past nine in the morning and I was still only fifteen, but I was about to start on the rum and Coke for breakfast. As I nodded over to Shafina, Donna huffed, turned around and stormed off into the kitchen. Shafina followed so I hung around in the living room as their argument intensified and reverberated off the kitchen walls. I tried not to eavesdrop, but I couldn't help myself. Some sentences were clearer than others as their argument travelled along the hallway and crept into the living room. It was clear that Shafina was trying to argue in whispers, but Donna's voice fired back at her fast and loud:

'No ... I'm sick of it .... you always say that ... I've had enough. No, I don't want a drink. You owe me ...'

Shafina was trying her best to be quiet, but I could hear as she hissed back at the young girl: 'Do as you're told ... being rude ... no, I won't. I'll play whatever I like. This is my flat ... well, you're free to leave any time you want ... there's the door!'

I imagined Shafina pointing at it – the two of them caught in a stalemate as Donna considered her options. Angry footsteps sounded in the hallway and grew louder as they marched towards me in the living room. I sat down quickly on the sofa, terrified that I'd be caught trying to earwig on their argument.

Donna pushed the door wide open and flopped down beside me, but she refused to make eye contact. Her body language – her whole demeanour – was totally defensive. Whatever the row had been about, it had to be something serious.

'I fucking hate her! Fat bitch!' she cursed under her breath, but still loudly enough for me to hear.

Donna had a Yorkshire accent, but she definitely didn't sound as though she came from Rotherham.

'She's a fucking bitch!' she cursed again, rolling her eyes skyward, clearly delighted that she had an audience.

I nodded knowingly.

'I get like that with my mum sometimes,' I lied, trying to make her feel better.

Donna turned sharply towards me.

'What, Shafina?'

The young girl began to laugh, although I didn't understand why. She continued to roar with laughter as I looked on, completely baffled.

Suddenly, a large shadow was cast inside the room as Shafina appeared in the doorway, blocking out the light from the hallway. She was a daunting woman in more ways than one.

'It's good to see you making friends for once, Donna,' Shafina snarled, her voice laced with sarcasm.

The teenager huffed and crossed both arms as Shafina stepped forward and handed me a drink and a plate of buttered toast. It was another rum and Coke, only this time I didn't sip it; I gulped it down until I'd drained my glass.

Donna seethed silently next to me. It was clear she was furious about something, but Shafina ignored her and focused all her attention on me.

'Ciggie?'

I wasn't sure what to do but Shafina didn't pause or wait for my answer. Instead, she sparked up a cigarette and handed it to me. I studied the cigarette burning between my fingers, the smoke curling upwards past my face and above my head. A few days ago, I didn't drink or smoke, but now I was doing both. However, I loved my new life and my new friends because they were just so … unpredictable, which is what made it all seem so exciting.

The rest of the day passed by without any more incidents. Donna stayed seated next to me, texting on her phone. It was obvious that she was still sulking, but I knew she wasn't angry with me, she was angry with her mum. Shafina seemed happy enough – jolly even – as though everything was perfectly fine as she passed me drink after drink. I'm not sure how much I'd had, but the walls felt as though they were leaning in towards me as I struggled to hold my head upright. When it eventually became too much, I allowed my head to flop forwards and rested the tip of my chin against my chest. My eyes closed and the room faded away.

I have to get out of here … fresh air … I need fresh air! the voice inside my brain screamed, thinking I was about to be sick.

I took a deep and panicked breath and suddenly I was back there, inside the room. Although I was awake, it felt as though I was still waiting for my legs to catch up with the rest of me. My whole body felt weird, as though it was made of plasticine. I narrowed my eyes and tried to focus on the wall opposite, but the room faded away to black. I'm not sure how long I was asleep but when I finally opened my eyes, Donna had shifted across the room. She was sitting next to Shafina as though the two were discussing a secret plan. I stared at her, but her expression was difficult to read.

She looks annoyed … no, it's not that … she looks concerned. I blinked hard and tried to focus. I *needed* to focus.

She seems concerned, but for who? Me? Her?

My brain felt sluggish and struggled to process everything. All I did know was that I had to stand up and I had to go home right now.

'Aww, you're not leaving already, are you?'

Shafina's voice cut across the room in waves as though life had suddenly switched into slow motion.

'I neeeeed … neeeed to gehhhht hommme,' I slurred, struggling to stand and trying to string a sentence together.

'Whoa! Be careful, El.'

Suddenly my legs betrayed me and I toppled over to one side. Thankfully, the sofa was there to catch me and I fell back down onto it, landing heavily.

'Maybe you should wait here a bit longer until you feel a bit steadier,' Shafina suggested.

I narrowed my eyes and tried to look at her, but her face drifted in and out of focus.

I blinked and rubbed the back of my hand against both eyes to try to keep her and the rest of the room still. I couldn't see her, but I imagined Donna's eyes burning into me, willing me to leave. Paranoia seemed to grip me.

Maybe she's jealous. Was that it? Did she think I was trying to come between her and her mum?

'I juusst neeed t'go …' I cringed as the words slurred again from my mouth.

I had to sober up before I returned home. My parents would kill me if they could see me like this. I had to get some fresh air.

'Here,' Shafina said, hooking a hand beneath my armpit to try to anchor me and lift me to my feet. 'Let me help you.'

I felt grateful to her, but I also desperately wanted to leave. The room was dark, too hot and claustrophobic.

Why are the windows covered with that net curtain and why doesn't she ever open them?

'Neeed to g-g-go.'

The hallway felt as though it was a thousand feet long as I staggered along it, placing my palms flat against the cool plaster to stop from crumpling down into a big heap.

Not much further. I can see the door …

The darkened hallway glowed with a sudden flash of light – sunshine – and it was coming from outside. She had opened the door. I wasn't sure how long I'd been in the flat, but outside it seemed to be the middle of the afternoon. I wondered why it had felt so much later.

'There you go,' Shafina smiled.

I felt a sudden warmth as she laid a concerned hand against my back to try to guide me.

'Mind how you go. See you again soon.'

I turned to face her; this mountain of a woman – a strange mixture of friend and something else.

Who is she and why is she always so nice to me?

Uncertainty crawled across my skin like a thousand insects, as though something was trying to alert me. Everything told me that this situation was anything but normal, but I refused to listen. Instead, I stepped outside, said goodbye and made my way home. The whole day felt surreal – like a long and strange dream.

The following morning, Shafina answered the door bright and early to let me in, only this time there were no smiles or laughter. Instead, she turned and marched back into the front room where she was in the middle of a vicious row with Donna. I did my best to try to lift the tension in the flat. I even tried to strike up a conversation with Donna, but as usual she was angry and aggressive. At one point, she stormed out of the room. When she finally reappeared, she seemed normal and calm. However, moments later, she lost her temper again and walked away from me.

What the hell is her problem?

A little while later, I decided to try again.

'So,' I began, 'I'm trying to place your accent. You sound like you're from Yorkshire, but you don't sound as though you're from Rotherham …'

Donna glanced up from her phone and considered me for a moment. My stomach clenched with nerves.

Is she going to answer or ignore me?

The girl locked her eyes on me.

'That's because I'm not from Rotherham.'

'Oh, I see.'

Although I didn't, not really.

She immediately glanced back down at her phone.

Say something else. Don't clam up now!

'So, er, did you always live with Shafina then?'

Donna lifted her head again, her face a mixture of annoyance and confusion.

'No, why do you say that? I lived in a hostel,' she snapped.

She stared at me as though she was waiting for an explanation. I scratched my head. Now it was my turn to be confused.

Why did she live in a hostel? It doesn't make any sense.

I needed to say more, so I did.

'Right,' I replied.

Is she lying?

'Sorry, it's just, I thought … I mean …'

She sat and waited for me to spit out what it was I was trying to say.

'Sorry, but how come you lived in a hostel when you've got a mum?'

Donna laughed. 'Mum? What are you on about? I didn't live with my mum,' she said, her voice rising a notch.

She was really starting to piss me off now.

'Yeah, but what I mean is, you live with Shafina now, don't you?' I responded.

Donna stared back at me as though I'd completely lost the plot. Her mouth gaped open as she began to shake her head in disbelief.

'What are you on about? You don't think … er, you don't mean? Shafina isn't my mum!' she said, guffawing.

But I still didn't understand and now I'd started I just couldn't leave it.

'Oh, right, what I mean is … erm, what I'm trying to say is, Shafina said she was …'

Donna looked up from her phone and stared at me blankly.

'... Erm,' I mumbled. 'It's just that Shafina said she was your mum.'

Donna continued to stare in disbelief as though her brain was struggling to compute what I'd just said. I was about to ask her more when there was a loud knock at the door. It was so sudden and unexpected that it startled us both.

'Come in!' Shafina's voice hollered from the kitchen as she walked along the hallway towards us and the living room. Donna immediately fixed her eyes on her phone and I knew right then that our conversation was over.

Shafina came into the living room and plonked herself on the sofa opposite. Donna didn't even look up. Instead, she stood up and moved over towards the window – a scowl still etched across her face. There was another argument brewing, I could feel it – like a thunderstorm – and I was certain it had something to do with what I'd just said.

The front door slammed and, moments later, a clean-shaven Pakistani man came into the living room. He was dressed in a grimy white T-shirt that strained across the paunch of his belly, blue jeans and trainers.

'Hi, Hazi,' Shafina said, smiling up at him as he paused in the doorway to check out who was in the room.

Hazi lifted a hand and waved over at Shafina before crossing to sit down next to me. I tried to shift along so that he wasn't too close. As I did, he slid over and bunched up next to me again. My heart sank. He was absolutely disgusting and stank of body odour. His hair was greasy and he wore it with a severe parting right down the middle; it hung like the curtains Shafina didn't own.

I leaned forward, picked up my drink and knocked it back in an attempt to try to numb myself. The strange man – Hazi – stared at me the whole time as though I was a box of treasure. I felt his eyes as they crawled all over me, sliding up and down my body. He leered and leched as though he'd never seen a young girl before. Thankfully, I'd already changed out of my school uniform. By now, I was coming to Shafina's prepared, with a pair of tracksuit bottoms and a T-shirt stashed inside my school bag. My trackie bottoms were Adidas, blue and white, but my trainers were always black Nike. It was trendy to mix up the labels so that stuff didn't match.

Hazi began to tell some awful jokes to try to make me laugh, but they were all corny and not very funny. I looked at Donna for back-up. She was standing over by the window but refused to look up. I was still staring over at her when Hazi began to tell me that he worked as a taxi driver. Although he was overweight and I guessed he looked much older than he actually was, I presumed that he must be in his early thirties. It was also obvious that he considered himself a bit of a ladies' man – a real catch – when actually he was anything but. Suddenly I felt a slight weight and warmth radiating from the inside of my thigh – Hazi's hand.

What the fuck is he doing? I thought as I jolted away from him.

'Oh, don't be scared!' he said, beginning to snigger as though it had been a joke.

But I was shocked and repulsed.

'Get off me!' I screamed, pushing him away angrily.

Hazi shrugged as though it was no big deal. I looked over to Shafina for her to say something, but she laughed.

What the fuck is going on here?

A short while later, she rose to her feet and announced that she was nipping to the kitchen to fetch more drinks.

'Another one, El?' she asked, shaking my empty glass.

I nodded. Anything to pass the time and try to blot out the creep sitting next to me.

But as soon as she had left the room, so did Donna. Suddenly, I found myself all alone as Hazi began to flirt with me clumsily.

Hurry up, Shafina. Please hurry up!

He made my skin prickle with panic. I was just about to stand up when Shafina came back into the room. In her hands were two drinks – one for me and one for her. I took the glass from her gratefully. I was just about to move to the sofa opposite but Shafina was faster than I was and claimed it first. Now I was stuck with Hazi. I inched along the sofa, the faux leather squeaking beneath me, which made him turn. I felt young, awkward and completely out of my depth.

Watch him, El. Watch him. Watch his hands …

The room fell silent as Shafina lit up a joint and passed it over to me and Hazi.

'You want some spliff, El?' she asked, blowing a lung-ful of bluish-grey smoke from her mouth.

I'd never tried drugs before but decided that they couldn't be that much different to cigarettes so I took it from her. I opened my mouth, placed the joint between my lips and took a long, exaggerated drag. I didn't want to look young and foolish in front of them. I wanted – no, *I needed* – Hazi to think that I was in control; that I knew exactly what I was doing and that I wouldn't take any crap.

'Whoa!' he cried. 'Leave some for me!'

Hazi began to laugh and then he winked at me as though we were best friends. His constant attention made me feel nauseous. Although, if truth be told, I couldn't be certain if it was him or the dope that made me feel that way. At first, I didn't think the spliff had had any effect, but then my head began to swim as my body pulsed with waves of overwhelming calm. The spliff, coupled with the drink, began to make me feel sick. I tried to slow things down and take only small sips of rum.

'So, what's a nice girl like you doing here?'

It was Hazi. He had leaned in close so he could whisper in my ear. His breath felt hot and sticky against my neck and I immediately backed away. Instead of being offended, Hazi chuckled.

'Right, top-ups. You two chat while I go get us some more drinks,' Shafina announced before swiftly exiting the room.

I found myself alone once more as Hazi continued to ogle me. I felt extremely uncomfortable; every time I tried to move, he'd squeeze up right next to me. It was relentless.

'So, why are you single?' he leered, snaking an arm along the sofa and behind my shoulders.

I sat upright and slid forward to the edge of my seat to try to escape him. The room felt claustrophobic with him in it; his clothes smelled cheesy, as though they'd not been aired properly after washing, and the cheap aftershave he had doused himself in caught at the back of my throat, choking me.

'I'm just … I'm going to see if Shafina needs any help in the kitchen,' I mumbled, trying to get to my feet.

Somehow, I managed to stand up and leave the room. I wandered along the hallway, passing my reflection in the mirror.

What the fuck are you doing? I thought as I noticed my bloodshot eyes and sallow skin. I looked sickly, as though I'd not slept for a week.

Carrying on down the hallway, I stumbled into the kitchen. Shafina was standing there – a fag in her mouth – searching through some drawers, trying to find a lighter. I watched as she tapped both hands against her tunic pockets and held them up in frustration.

'There must be one somewhere … have you seen it?'

I shook my head.

'No, Shafina, listen. Who's that in there?'

She glanced up, the unlit fag dangling from the corner of her mouth. 'Who? Hazi?'

I nodded.

'Yeah, him.'

'Why?'

She opened and closed each drawer, her hand exploring every one, still searching for her elusive lighter.

I leaned back against the kitchen work surface.

'It's just, erm … don't you think he's a bit, er, odd?'

She stopped searching, straightened up and looked at me properly for the very first time.

'Odd? What do you mean?'

I panicked a little because I suddenly realised how rude I sounded. After all, I was standing inside her flat, drinking her drink and now I'd just insulted one of her friends.

'Oh, I don't know. I just don't feel …' I said, trying to find the right words. 'Comfortable. That's it, I don't feel comfortable with him. I'm sorry, Shafina, but I don't like him. I mean, I don't like being left alone with him.'

She looked at me and shook her head as though I was overreacting.

'Oh, there's nothing wrong with Hazi. He's a nice lad. He's harmless. Give him a chance. You'll soon like him when you get to know him. You just need to get to know him.'

I nodded reluctantly, even though I was certain I could never feel comfortable with someone like Hazi.

'Sorry,' I mumbled a little later, apologising for not liking her friend.

Shafina shrugged it off.

'It's okay. But he's a good lad, El. You should get to know him; I promise you'll get to like him.'

In spite of their vicious argument when I'd first arrived at the flat, Donna reappeared and seemed to have calmed down. Occasionally she'd spit out the odd barbed comment, but it was nothing I hadn't heard before.

Soon it was 6 p.m. and I was late, even by my standards. I knew there would be questions back at home because my parents would want to know where I'd been.

'Aww, you're leaving already?' Hazi said, lifting a hand to try to grab and pull me back down. I moved away swiftly before he could.

'I'd better go,' I said, turning to speak to Shafina.

Donna was wandering around the flat, but I didn't know where she was.

'Bye, Donna!' I called.

I waited for her reply, but I was met with silence.

Thinking that she must be sulking yet again, I quickly changed back into my school uniform, then went to the front door and closed it behind me.

As soon as I reached home, Mum was waiting to speak to me.

'Where have you been? I've been worried sick.'

'Out. I've been out,' I said, brushing past her.

'Yes, but who with?'

'I told you,' I said, rolling my eyes. 'I've been out with mates.'

'What mates?'

'Mates. Mates from school. You don't know them so there's no point …' I huffed.

Then I stropped upstairs and disappeared into my bedroom. I'd decided that if Mum pressed me further, I'd tell her I'd been out with a friend called Donna. It was close enough to the truth.

The following day, instead of going to school, I headed straight for Shafina's place. It was still early morning, but she welcomed me inside and immediately poured me a large rum and Coke. I glanced around the kitchen, checked in the bathroom and then in the living room. The place felt eerily quiet. Then I realised.

'Where's Donna?' I enquired, as I flopped down onto the sofa.

'Who?' Shafina replied.

I half laughed, thinking she was winding me up.

'Donna. Where is she? Is she out?'

Shafina took a huge gulp from her glass, placed it on the table and pulled out a packet of cigarettes as I waited – waited for ages for her to answer.

'She's gone,' Shafina replied bluntly and without a hint of emotion.

She popped a cigarette in her mouth, pulled out a lighter and clicked it; the yellow flame began to dance as she lit the end.

I didn't understand.

'Gone. What do you mean? Where has she gone?'

The embers of Shafina's cigarette glowed orange as she inhaled a lungful of smoke. She held it inside and considered me for a moment. Then she released a long plume of blue-grey smoke.

'I don't know, El. All I know is she's gone and she's not coming back.'

She picked up her drink off the cluttered coffee table and drained it in one go. Then she grunted as she clambered to her feet.

'Another drink?' she asked, shaking the empty glass.

I nodded but inside my mind was whirring.

Why has Donna left and where has she gone?

Despite further questions from me throughout the rest of the day, Shafina refused to be drawn on Donna. If anything, whenever I mentioned her name, she seemed to clam up and declined to say any more. To Shafina, the girl was as good as dead.

I never saw Donna again after that day. I didn't realise it then, but I had unwittingly just become her replacement.

CHAPTER FOUR

THE KITCHEN

'Right,' I said, checking the time on my mobile phone. 'I'd better go.'

Donna had been gone a fortnight, and since then I had called at Shafina's flat every day, and had begun to stay overnight every so often. With the older teenager no longer on the scene, it made things easier somehow. For a start, the horrible tension and vicious arguments between the two had vanished with her. Not that I had a clue where she had gone or why, because Shafina refused to be drawn on it; all she would say was that Donna had always been a 'moody cow' and that she was glad to see the back of her.

As soon as I stood up to leave, Shafina gripped her stomach and began to complain.

'What's wrong?' I gasped as she rolled around on the sofa clutching her back and lower belly with both hands.

'Owwww ...' she moaned, crying out loud and cradling her large belly.

'What is it ...? What's wrong? Can I get you anything?' I asked, the panic rising in my voice.

drink earlier; the bitter aftertaste was still there and it felt tacky against my tongue.

Satisfied, Hazi zipped up his jeans as I curled into a protective ball. I scanned the floor for my clothes and spotted my navy-blue trackie bottoms and knickers, which I'd kicked off during the struggle, lying on the carpet. My underwear had a teddy-bear pattern on it – they were the same knickers that Mum had bought me only a few months ago. My stomach somersaulted with horror. Mum.

What would she think if she could see me now?

I wondered what she was doing right now and if she was at work or at home with Dad. I desperately wanted to see them again, but I knew Shafina wouldn't allow it.

'They don't care about you. If they did, they would have come and got you by now,' she reminded me. 'They don't love you like I do. We're a team, El, and teams stick together. I've got your back and you've got mine. You belong here with me. Look at everything I've done for you.'

But deep down, I knew that Shafina didn't have my back, because she hadn't protected me against Don or Hazi. It was only a matter of time before another stranger called at the flat and raped me, or worse. I had been conditioned to be compliant. Shafina had already made it perfectly clear that I owed her. I was her property now.

A few days after the rape, I was alone and dozing on the sofa. I felt so out of it that I was certain Shafina had drugged my drink again. I was so far gone that I couldn't feel a thing and I knew that nothing could touch me. The pain of the rapes was already there – the worst had already happened. Afterwards, I felt nothing but shame and disgust. The only thing I didn't feel was anger.

I closed my eyes. I needed to sleep and time to think. I had to get away, but I didn't know how to do it or where I'd go. I recalled the graffiti on the windows.

NONCE.

PAEDOPHILE.

Shafina had refused to tell me what the words meant, but I realised they must have been something bad because someone – an enemy of Shafina's – had smashed the window with a brick. I was still mulling it over when I slipped into a deep sleep and allowed my body to give way to a drug-induced exhaustion. My arms flopped down by my sides as the softness of the sofa swallowed me whole.

'El … El!'

My eyelids fluttered because I recognised the voice. There was the sound of banging, as though someone was hammering something in the distance.

'Are you in there, El?'

Dad. It was my father's voice. I wasn't sure if I was dreaming as I listened again.

BANG, BANG, BANG!

'El!' the voice shouted.

'I'm here, I'm in here, Dad!' I tried to cry out but there was something stopping me – something clamped against my mouth.

Here, Dad. I'm here!

It was as if my voice had been stolen from me. I tried to concentrate. Was he really here? Was it my father or was it all in my head?

There was a light tap against my shoulder. I turned.

'Dad?' I sobbed.

I wept tears of joy as my father held me in his arms and cradled me as though I was a little girl.

'Aren't you angry?' I asked him.

He shook his head.

'Don't be silly, we love you …'

My tears blinded me as I tried to look up at him. Dad had come for me, just as he always had.

I was little again and I was running through a playground when I tripped and fell. The skin had scuffed away from my knee and I watched in fascination as pinpricks of blood rose to the surface in a red speckled pattern. Dad knelt down and checked my wound …

BANG, BANG, BANG!

'Let me in … I want to see my daughter!'

There it was again, the thud of a fist or was it a foot? The sound of thumping. Suddenly there was a shift in the air and I sensed someone standing close by. Someone was there …

'Dad?'

My mind felt fuggy and disoriented, as though someone had picked me up and shaken me like a snow globe. As my scattered thoughts slowly floated back down to earth and settled, I thought I heard more voices – men's voices.

'Come with us.'

There was the sound of a disturbance – a scuffle.

'Don't want to … my daughter … get her home …'

Dad?

But the voice thinned until soon there was nothing left, only an empty silence.

A large hand pressed against the top of my arm, as though someone was trying to rouse me.

'Dad?'

I rose quickly, as though coming up for air, and opened my eyes. I'd expected to find him standing in front of me, but every part of me shrank with disappointment when I realised it wasn't Dad, it was Shafina.

'Wake up, it's just a bad dream, El. You were talking in your sleep,' she said, her moon-shaped face looming into view.

Bitter disappointment surged through me; my mind or the drugs she'd spiked my drink with had been playing tricks on me. The warmth of embarrassment flooded my face. Shafina had seen it all. She'd heard me, and now I felt a fool.

'Right, okay,' I mumbled.

My head throbbed in protest as I pulled myself upright on the sofa. Dad's voice had sounded so clear, as though he'd been standing just feet away from me. However, when I mentioned it a little later, Shafina just laughed.

'It's just your mind playing tricks on you, El. I told you. They don't care about you like I do. That's why you need to stay here.'

Dream or not, it had all felt so real.

CHAPTER ELEVEN

THE PARK

It was mid-afternoon when I heard the door slam. A man I'd never seen before appeared in the doorway. Shafina glanced up, clearly delighted to see him.

The stranger was small and Iranian, as I was later told, and he introduced himself as a neighbour.

'Ervin!' she gushed, rising to her feet. 'Come in, come in!'

The man hovered in the doorway and smiled over at me.

'I live upstairs,' he said, by way of explanation.

'Have you brought it?' Shafina asked, butting in; her eyes were wide and expectant.

Ervin nodded before turning back to face me.

'My name is Ervin. In Persia this means friend of honour,' he explained, tapping a hand against his heart proudly.

'El,' I replied curtly.

I was unimpressed by him and his name.

Shafina watched as he dug a hand inside his trouser pocket and pulled something out; it was a small, round green bottle.

'Hang on,' she said, stopping him. 'I'll go and fetch a spoon.'

I didn't have a clue what was in the bottle or what it was they were about to do. Instead, I looked on in fascination. A moment later, she had returned with a tablespoon. She led Ervin into the living room and he proceeded to pour some brown liquid onto the spoon. Once it had been filled to the brim, Shafina placed the spoon against her mouth and tipped the liquid inside, drinking it. Ervin poured a second spoonful as Shafina sank into the sofa next to him. Then he did the same. I watched the two of them as their eyes rolled inside their heads. They were still awake, but both seemed completely out of it. The room was silent because apart from the odd murmur, they stayed that way – comatose – for the rest of the day. I wasn't sure if they were okay, but I continued to watch; I wondered what on earth they had taken to render them both almost unconscious. Hours passed before Shafina began to fidget and move; she was finally coming around. Then Ervin did the same. As they both regained consciousness, the male neighbour began to flirt with Shafina, who laughed and playfully slapped a hand against his chest. It was obvious that something was either going on between them or had happened in the not-too-distant past. Apart from the flirting, Shafina and Ervin had spent most of the afternoon in silence. Eventually, Ervin clambered to his feet and bade her farewell.

'Bye,' she said, still smiling as he left the room.

Then the front door slammed. We were alone again. Still curious, I turned to Shafina because there were a million questions I wanted to ask her.

'What was that stuff?'

She sighed, as though still a little dazed and confused. 'What stuff?'

'That stuff – the stuff he poured on the spoon.'

She paused for a moment, considering her answer.

'I take it for my endometriosis. You know how much I suffer.'

I shook my head.

'Yeah, I get that bit, but what is it – the stuff?'

She looked over and shifted uneasily in her seat.

'Opium.'

And that was it, the end of our conversation. I didn't know what opium was, but after witnessing the pair of them, I made a mental note never to try it.

Later that evening there was a loud knock at the door. Shafina pulled herself up off the sofa and went to answer it.

'She's just through here,' I heard her say as she showed a man through into the living room.

I glanced up.

'Hi,' the man said, staring over at me.

In that moment, my stomach seemed to fall away. He was Asian, just like Hazi and Don.

I wonder if she'll expect you to have sex with him as well.

'All right,' I mumbled half-heartedly.

By now, I was becoming accustomed to all the comings and goings at Shafina's flat; the strange men who wanted to paw and use me for whatever they wanted. I expected the man to sit down, only he didn't. Instead, he remained standing. Something was different.

'Come on, El,' Shafina said, waving her hand, urging me to stand up.

'Come on for what?'

Just then, I realised how much I sounded like Donna; I'd become just like her.

Had she been trapped like me?

Donna had disappeared without any warning. I'd always wondered what had happened to make her leave so quickly. As soon as I thought about it, another thought occurred to me. It was so awful that it made me shiver.

Was Donna even still alive?

It seemed so utterly ridiculous that I shook it immediately from my head.

Yes, of course she was!

'Well ...' Shafina barked impatiently, clicking her fingers as though I was a dog. 'He's waiting ...'

'Yeah, sorry ...'

'In a world of her own, this one,' she said by way of an apology to the stranger.

The man looked to be in his thirties and, unlike Hazi, was clean-shaven and smartly dressed. He wore trendy blue jeans and a designer grey T-shirt, and his hair was super neat and closely shaved at the sides.

'This is Dav,' Shafina said by way of introduction. 'He's going to take you out for a bit.'

Out? I never go out!

In fact, I hadn't left Shafina's flat for days ... weeks? I didn't even know because I'd lost track of time living in the half-light of her flat; one day simply blurred into another, and the longer I stayed, the more elastic time seemed to become.

'Out?' I mumbled, repeating her.

'Yes, that's right. Now, off you go. Go on, off with the pair of you,' she insisted, shooing us into the hallway.

I felt the firm push of a hand against the small of my back as she steered me towards Dav and the front door. As I walked along the narrow hallway, I caught my reflection in the large mirror.

You look dead behind the eyes, I thought as I spotted my reflection.

'Have fun!' Shafina chirped and then she slammed the door behind us.

THUD!

Outside, the air felt cold. The sky was an inky dark blue, studded with tiny stars. It was actually the middle of the night, but I hadn't even realised. The orange street lamp illuminated Dav as he climbed the small concrete steps outside Shafina's flat. He turned left, walked around the building and headed towards the main road. I followed and spotted a large black hackney cab parked up outside.

'Get in,' he said, nodding over at it.

His face was unsmiling as fear rose at the back of my throat like vomit. I was absolutely petrified. But I was too scared to refuse, so I did as he'd asked. I'd been systematically groomed to follow orders and my life had become anything but normal, so I pulled the chrome handle until the door clicked open, then slid onto the back seat. As I did, Dav climbed into the front and sat behind the steering wheel. Even though we were separated by a flimsy glass screen, I felt his eyes on me the whole time; I caught him staring, watching through the interior mirror. The cab momentarily jolted forward as the engine started. Dav released the brake and we pulled silently away from the kerb into the night. To a casual bystander, I would have looked like any other young girl, catching a cab to provide a safe passage home. Only this journey was anything but that.

Perched on the edge of the black leather seat, my body slid with every sharp corner he negotiated. I decided to fasten the seat belt around me, even though I knew it could only protect me from so much. Leaning against the car window, I used my hand to wipe away the silvery condensation and stared out at the blackened night. My eyes scoured the scene outside, looking for clues as to where we were. I was searching for something familiar, but I didn't recognise anything. Instead, the car whizzed by rows of unfamiliar identical houses, all with the same matchbox-sized front gardens. Their shadows linked together in a bizarre grey daisy chain.

I tried to swallow but a nervous lump had filled the back of my throat. Anxiety. I gulped again and pressed my face against the small, cold window. I watched as a stream of orange lights blurred into a long stream of electric neon. It glowed brightly against the night. It was early spring and still cold, but at least it wasn't raining. My nerves jangled as each breath I took grew faster, my lungs powered by my thumping heart.

Where the hell is he taking you?

Other traffic brought me comfort because I knew there were people out there – potential witnesses, should he do me harm. At one point, Dav pulled the car to a halt at a red light and ratcheted on the handbrake.

Run, run! the voice screamed.

He was still watching me. His eyes flicked, alternating between the road and me. I turned so that he couldn't read my face as a plan began to form inside my mind.

Do it! Run! Pull the handle. If you're quick, you could escape!

My eyes looked to the right. The car door handle was situated just above my lap. I wondered how long it would take for me to open it and climb out. I was still wondering when I spotted a small, glowing red dot.

RED LIGHT INDICATES THE DOORS ARE SECURED, a sign next to it read.

Shit!

I slumped back in my seat and tried to look confident. I didn't feel it. My eyes glanced at him through the same oblong mirror that hung from the car ceiling, slightly to the left of his head. Suddenly his eyes met mine.

'All right?'

'Yeah,' I replied, sounding more confident than I felt.

He's going to park up somewhere and rape you! the voice inside my head warned.

Nausea rose up and scorched the back of my throat as my body rattled with fear. I was on high alert. This hadn't been a chance encounter; this had been arranged in advance and Shafina was behind it all.

Outside, more unfamiliar landscape whizzed by as my panic mounted. The longer we drove, the more convinced I became that Dav's motives were entirely sinister.

He's taking you somewhere secluded so he can rape you. He might even kill you!

My breathing grew laboured; I tried to summon up enough courage to strike up a conversation to get on the good side of him.

'Where are we going?' I asked.

His eyes darted from the road and met mine in the mirror.

'You'll see.'

His reply felt ominous and it left me with more questions than answers.

'Oh,' I replied, trying to sound casual. 'It's just that I don't recognise where we are.'

There was a silence and for a moment I wondered if he'd turned off the intercom connecting the front and passenger seats. However, a slight crackle sounded and then he spoke.

'You'll recognise it soon enough.'

The taxi navigated a few more corners until eventually he indicated and pulled off the main road into a heavily wooded area. I was terrified as I stared through the glass, looking for a road sign or anything, but there was nothing. I steeled myself.

This is it; this is where he rapes you. This is where he will dump your body.

In my mind's eye I was already dead, my body pressed against the cold earth. My mouth was closed but there was a fine coating of dark soil against my lips; both my lungs were deflated and had been emptied, with no breath left. I was as cold as the earth he'd abandoned me on.

'Almost there.'

The unexpected sound of his voice made me jump.

Then another thought.

Does he have a weapon?

I hadn't noticed one, but then I hadn't expected to leave Shafina's flat and be driven to God only knew where in the middle of the night.

'It's just down here,' he said, interrupting my panic, as the cab jolted along a single-lane dirt track.

My body bounced up and down, feeling every bump. We were deep in the woods and surrounded by trees on both sides; their branches arched together above the cab roof, enclosing us, like entwined fingers. The foliage camouflaged and hid us away from the rest of the world.

This is it.

I took a deep breath.

Strangle. That's what he'll do, he'll strangle you. He won't need a weapon for that …

My imagination went into overdrive as I pictured what was yet to come. Finally, the car turned and swung into what looked like a parking bay. Dav parked up and snuffed out the headlights, plunging us both into complete darkness.

'That's it, we're here.'

My eyes scanned the forest outside.

'But where … where are we?'

I was still peering outside, with my face pressed against the window and my body glued to the seat. I didn't want to leave what now felt like the safe confines of his cab.

'The park – we're at the park,' Dav said, undoing his seat belt.

Christ! He's going to rape and murder you in the park!

'Which park?' I asked, desperately trying to recall all the parks in the area.

My brain worked quickly, trying to formulate an escape route. I calculated that we'd only been travelling for ten minutes, which meant we were either still in or near Rotherham.

If you run now then you might make it to a nearby house … even a police station. You could ask for help …

'Thrybergh. We're at Thrybergh Country Park,' he said, cutting through my panic.

I didn't know Thrybergh well, but I knew one thing – it was absolutely bloody massive!

You could run and hide in the trees ... wait for him to leave.

Possible escape routes and scenarios whirred around inside my brain.

'Come on, follow me,' he said, offering me his arm, like a gentleman.

But I didn't want to link arms because I wanted to know why the hell he'd brought me to a park in the middle of the night. For a change, I was stone-cold sober. I'd had a drink earlier but the cold night air and the impromptu trip in Dav's cab had wiped away any intoxication. In some ways, I almost wished I was drunk because at least then I knew I wouldn't feel anything. I certainly wouldn't be as shit scared as I was right now.

'Where are we going?'

My body trembled as I followed him into the woods. My heart clattered beneath my ribcage as he led me along a well-trodden woodland path. I made a mental note of each bush and unusually shaped tree so that I might be able to use them later as a landmark. It seemed even darker beneath a roof of treetops. The only light was the moon, which peeked intermittently through the gaps in the branches. I lifted my head skywards as the leaves shivered and rustled against the breeze.

No one will hear you scream. No one.

There were unusual noises that startled me. I turned, on full alert.

'What was that?'

Dav chuckled to himself.

'Probably just an owl.'

But I wasn't convinced.

Were there more men waiting for me?

Spindly branches cracked beneath our feet as I heard other sounds – woodland creatures. I wondered if they were watching us. But there would be no other witnesses.

Unless there are more.

The trees continued to sway above our heads. Although they were cast in shadow, some of them looked darker and denser with leaves and life.

Life. Would he let me live?

'Come on, not far now,' Dav said, trying to hurry me up.

Only I didn't want to hurry up; I wanted to be back at Shafina's flat. I wanted to be safe, not here with this stranger – a man I'd never met before. I shivered with both cold and fear. I rubbed my hands against the tops of my arms to try to revive my frozen skin. My T-shirt and thin tracksuit top were no match for the plunging night-time temperature. Shafts of moonlight continued to peek through the gaps above until slowly it revealed itself as a complete circle and we emerged into a large clearing.

'Over here,' Dav called, beckoning me to follow.

Reluctantly, I walked behind him along the path. At least we were out of the woods. Trailing in his footsteps, I tried to size him up. Dav was slim but so much taller than me. I knew that even if I ran, he'd definitely catch me.

Wait. Bide your time. Wait until he's distracted, then run.

He strolled over towards a park bench and sat down. The bench overlooked a large lake, which rippled black beneath the moonlight, making it feel even more ominous. Tapping his hand against the metal slats, he encouraged me to take a seat next to him. My body felt heavy, as though made of concrete. I wanted to slow things down to try to buy myself extra time – time to escape before he raped or murdered me.

Looking all around, I realised that it was hopeless – there was nowhere to hide, only water.

My knees buckled as I fell onto the bench next to him. My arms and legs prickled with goosebumps as both my palms began to sweat. I wiped them against the knees of my tracksuit bottoms.

This is it – get ready.

I waited, but nothing happened. I waited some more, my eyes intermittently darting towards him, waiting for the slightest movement, but nothing happened. Dav didn't lunge at me. In fact, he didn't even turn or look my way. Instead, he began to speak.

Thud, thud, thud.

My heart sounded loudly as it hammered against my ribcage, reminding me to stay focused. Reminding me to run.

'So, how are you?' he asked, looking straight ahead.

'F-fine,' I stuttered.

My quivering voice betrayed my nerves, but Dav nodded.

'And what do you like doing?'

This is it. This is where he turns the conversation to sex.

I shook my head and tried to think, tried to buy extra time.

'What do you mean?'

He chuckled to himself as though enjoying a private joke.

'I mean, what do you like to do when you're not at Shafina's?'

My mind raced.

What do I like to do?

I couldn't even remember. My face must have looked a little blank because he decided to elaborate.

'I mean, the cinema. Do you like going to the cinema? Do you have any hobbies?'

Cinema. The word made me flinch because that's how Don had started all this ... he'd mentioned taking me to the cinema.

'No, I don't like the cinema,' I replied sharply.

I hoped it might put off whatever plans he had for me. I felt vulnerable and scared as I looked down at my lap; I realised that both of my hands were shaking. Placing them palms downwards, I wrapped my fingers around the edge of the metal seat to stop them from trembling. My arms were bent slightly at the elbows – my body poised and ready to run.

The moonlight reflected off Dav's face and I realised just how well groomed he was. His hair was cut in a short back and sides, his clothes were neat and he seemed remarkably calm, almost professional.

'What's Dav short for?'

I'd decided that I would turn the tables and ask him a few questions.

Dav's mouth broke into a wide smile as he shook his head.

'It doesn't matter.'

He was friendly but dismissive, as though I wasn't allowed to ask any questions.

'What do you do?' I said, trying to change tack.

'Taxi. I drive a taxi.'

I didn't believe him.

You're the smartest-looking taxi driver I've ever seen.

'What, in Rotherham?' I asked, pressing him for more details.

He shook his head.

'No, I tend to do airport runs.'

Again, I didn't believe a word of it. In my experience, black hackney cabs tended to be used for street pick-ups, not long airport runs. There was something about him that didn't ring true.

Without warning, he dipped sideways and leaned in towards me. I flinched and he noticed.

'Sorry, I was just going to say, I like your trainers,' he remarked, pointing down at them.

We both considered my feet. The black trainers weren't anything special, only Nike.

'Thanks.'

Another awkward pause followed until Dav spoke again.

'So, what music do you like?'

'Me? Anything. What about you?'

He shook his head as though he couldn't think of anything.

'Same.'

The conversation stuttered to a halt; it had been long and uncomfortable, with no real purpose or direction. After forty minutes or so, Dav stood up and turned to face me. I was unsure what to do so I waited.

This is it.

Bile had risen into the back of my mouth as my stomach churned with anxiety.

'Come on then,' he said, walking away towards the woods.

My blood chilled as my veins seemed to flood with ice-cold panic.

This is it – this is where he murders you. Why else would he have brought you here, to the middle of nowhere?

Slowly, I got up and followed him, but I was sure to stay five or so feet behind him at all times. Enough distance to make a run for it. Warily, I trailed him back into the dense woods.

Watch him – he might turn. This nice-guy stuff is just an act.

My heart continued to pound and my mouth was bone dry as we made our way deeper into the forest.

Over there – that's where he'll murder you. It's nice and dark there. No one will see. No one will hear you scream.

'Come on, keep up.'

Dav was way ahead of me now.

'Coming,' I called.

I continued to follow until suddenly we were back at the car park.

Thank God!

I let the nervous breath I'd been holding inside come rushing out of my lungs as a sigh of relief.

Dav walked over to the cab, unlocked it and took his place behind the steering wheel.

'Come on, hop in, I've got to get you back.'

Get me back?

I almost wept with relief, but my instincts told me not to relax – not just yet. Experience told me that was never just it; there was always someone or something waiting in the wings. I pulled the door handle and climbed into the back seat. As I did, the door clicked, locking me in as he started up the engine. The red dot glowed again, reminding me that there was no escape, not anymore. It was too late. The taxi crawled slowly out of the park until we had re-joined more familiar tarmacked roads. Soon, the outline of the dark daisy-chain houses reappeared and the reassuring glow of street lamps followed. Luminosity from the street lamps flooded the inside of the cab, colouring the black seats a dull shade of orange. My breathing relaxed and slowly began to return to normal because we were back in civilisation.

There's still time. Don't trust him. Be careful.

We turned corner after corner and eventually the familiar scenery of my neighbourhood loomed into view. A few moments later, we had turned into the main road that ran alongside Shafina's flat. The cab slowed as Dav pulled up against the kerb. I finally allowed myself to relax. Dav hadn't murdered me and left me for dead, he'd not raped or even tried to attack me. If anything, he'd been the perfect gentleman. Although I had learned, from bitter experience, that whenever I'd allowed myself to trust in the past, bad things had always happened. Only not tonight. Tonight, I survived.

The light of the red dot blinked off, signalling that my door was now unlocked. Seizing the chance, I grabbed the handle, pulled it towards me and pushed the cab door open. My legs were still trembling as I stepped down onto the pavement outside. With a short beep, Dav pressed the key fob, locked the cab and walked around the back of the building to Shafina's flat. He pushed the handle and opened the door, but he didn't go inside. Instead, she ran over towards him in greeting.

'Oh, you're back!' she gushed.

It was obvious from the look on her face that she was surprised we had returned so soon.

Even though she'd opened the door, Dav remained standing on the doormat outside. I pushed past them both silently until I was inside the hallway. Shafina didn't acknowledge me. Instead, she stared at Dav and held out her hand, as though waiting for some sort of payment.

Standing behind her, I turned to watch. Dav put his hand inside the pocket of his jeans and pulled out a single packet of cigarettes – Benson & Hedges Gold – Shafina's favourites. But there was something else in the palm of his hand. It was a long, thin plastic key for the electricity meter.

'Here,' he said, handing it over to her.

Shafina snatched it from his hand greedily.

'It's fully loaded with credit, so it should last you,' he explained, before turning and walking off into the night.

Shafina closed the door, but I had already vanished into the living room.

An hour or so later, we were sitting in silence in the front room when I decided to broach the subject.

'Was that a key for the meter? The electricity meter?' I asked, looking directly at her.

Shafina narrowed her eyes as she considered both me and my question.

'What if it was?' she said defensively.

I shrugged as though I didn't care.

'Oh, nothing. I just thought you'd give him some money for it.'

Her face clouded with fury and she shook her head as though it was none of my business.

'No, it's all sorted,' she insisted, signalling that the subject was now closed.

I now knew without doubt: the key and the fags had both been payment for me and for tonight. Once again, Shafina had sold me for little more than a packet of cigarettes. It was all she thought I was worth.

CHAPTER TWELVE

THE VISIT

Following my trip to the park with Dav, there was one thought that I just couldn't shake.

Why hadn't he tried anything on?

Although I'd been relieved, ever since I had been left utterly baffled. Hazi and Don had always expected something in return. Also, why had Dav asked me so many questions? I mulled it over until something struck me. In fact, it was so obvious that I cursed myself for not having realised it earlier.

His clothes, his professional manner … was he a police officer?

He had certainly looked and acted like one with his short back and sides. But what on earth would a police officer be doing mixing with the likes of Shafina, and why had he been driving a taxi?

It didn't matter how many times I tried to think it through, I kept coming to the same conclusion.

Then I remembered the other officer – the one who called Shafina every week.

Is Dav his colleague?

If so, why would a police officer be friendly with Shafina when she had encouraged me to have sex with older men, drink and take drugs. I was a child, and that was illegal, wasn't it? Also, why would a police officer take a fifteen-year-old girl to the park in the middle of the night? Nothing made sense.

Soon, I was caught up in a cycle. I had been raped by Hazi and Don. My life became blurred at the edges – a carousel of drink, drugs and sex. Although I wasn't drinking or smoking any more than usual, I felt different. Normally, Shafina would pour our drinks, and yet she never did this in front of me. Recently, I had suffered quite a few blackouts and complete memory blanks. I already suspected that she was adding more than just rum to my cola. She had to be drugging me, but what with? Then I remembered the liquid opium.

Has she been using that?

I could only judge it by how much I had seemed to be affected. Lately, I had felt as if my legs had no bones. Instead, they became weakened and unreliable; my sense of balance had also been off-kilter. On more than one occasion I'd struggled to stay awake. Often, I would open my eyes to find Hazi or Shafina sitting opposite, watching me. Sometimes I felt like a specimen inside a zoo. Even a normal day would be filled with blurred fragments and snippets of memories and conversations. But were they real or imagined? Almost overnight, my brain became a sieve, allowing smaller details to leak away and be instantly forgotten. Trying to retain any information whatsoever was challenging as I struggled to concentrate. Their faces would blur into nothingness as Hazi and Don raped me – all with Shafina's full knowledge. No normal woman or mother would allow that to happen in her flat, but then Shafina wasn't like any other woman. Instead, she existed in a seedy underworld of drugs, drink and darkness. She didn't let anyone or even daylight penetrate her world. Despite visits from Hazi and Don, it was just me and her locked inside the flat, away from the rest of the world. I had no sense of how long I'd been living there because without a point of focus – natural daylight or darkness – time had no structure.

So when I heard a knock at the door one day while Shafina was in the bathroom, I answered it while still half asleep. Standing on the doorstep was a woman in her forties. She was almost as wide as she was tall – a ball of a woman – and someone I'd never seen before. The woman introduced herself as PC Barron and explained that she was a police child protection officer, although she certainly didn't look like one – she was dressed in casual trousers and a shirt, and I found her manner abrupt to the point of rudeness.

'Hello,' she began formally.

I squinted my eyes against the bright afternoon sun and lifted a hand to shield my face.

Am I in trouble?

'Are you Elizabeth Harper?'

'Yes.'

'What are you doing?' she asked sharply.

Her body language was so defensive that it immediately put me on edge.

'Nothing to do with you,' I snapped.

'I've come to see if you are okay,' she explained, her voice softening a little.

It was obvious, just from looking at me, that I was anything but.

'Do I look all right?' I retorted, my voice laced with sarcasm.

Shafina appeared by my side. Her face was all wide-eyed and innocent. My eyes flitted between both women, who were waiting for my answer.

'I'm fine,' I insisted, as Shafina's body pressed close against mine.

The female police officer didn't say another word; instead, she shrugged her shoulders and walked off. I was incensed. She had called at the door and asked for me, but her whole demeanour had been wrong. Her approach left me baffled. How did she think I would answer her questions when she had spoken to me like that? Just like Dav at the park, her visit left me completely stumped. It felt as though she was just going through the motions.

I wasn't aware of it then, but my parents later said they had called the police over 800 times, begging them to rescue me from Shafina's flat, and that had been the response – to send that woman. By this time, I'd been living there for almost two months and my parents were frantic with worry.

As I went to close the door, I realised that I really did want to leave. I wanted to tell the female officer that I was trapped with Shafina and that she was mad. I wanted to tell her that Shafina played the same bloody song sixteen times a day and would sing along to it. I wanted to tell her all about Hazi and Don, and the rapes. I wanted to tell her everything. I wanted to do it right now – to leave and never look back. But with Shafina standing next to me, my courage failed me. I was too scared. There was a cool breeze and it blew against my face, sobering me slightly. Shafina's eyes were burning into me, willing me to shut the door so that we could get back to life as normal, whatever normal was. In a bizarre way, I felt sorry for her. I couldn't leave her because she had no one else, only me. I felt a misplaced loyalty to her, too. She had offered me a place to live when I'd felt lost, and now I was indebted to her – I belonged to her. I belonged to them all and I couldn't go home. Every sinew of my body told me to leave, but my brain refused. This world might be shit, but it was what I was used to and all I felt I deserved.

I paused in the doorway a moment longer, watching the police officer – my only chance of escape – leave. As I watched, I felt a warm hand rest against my spine.

'Good girl, El.'

Shafina took the edge of the door from my hands and closed it.

'Another drink?'

It was the last thing I needed. But she had already disappeared into the kitchen to make up another potion to numb and sedate me. Right now, that felt more than welcome. I was still thinking about the police officer when Shafina popped her head around the corner of the kitchen door and smiled brightly.

'I'll make it – you go and sit down in the living room. Hazi will be here soon, and he'll be looking forward to seeing you!'

My heart plummeted like a lead weight as I turned towards the darkened living room, the sofa and my prison.

* * *

The police child protection officer's visit had been prompted by my parents. I found out later that Mum had been so desperate that she had reported herself to the social services in a bid to push the authorities into action. I had even been assigned a woman from the local council called Yvonne. Social services had assessed Mum, who had passed and therefore I wasn't considered to be 'at risk'. This meant the authorities didn't have to do anything, even though I'd been missing from home for the best part of two months. Instead, South Yorkshire Police (SYP) raided my parents' house to check that they hadn't killed me. You couldn't make it up.

Around this time, my dad rented a council garage, so other officers from SYP made him unlock it to check that I wasn't hiding or had been buried in there. Even though my parents had told the police exactly where I was because, unbeknown to me, Mum had previously followed me. Although South Yorkshire Police had even sent out one of their own child protection officers to check on me, it continued to raid our home address in the middle of the night. Detectives would turn up unannounced and make my parents and younger sister stand aside while they rifled through all of our things. It was utter madness, yet in spite of my parents' protests, the hundreds of logged calls and the fact that I had answered Shafina's door to a female officer, SYP suspected my family of foul play and failed to offer any real help. There was, it seemed, no joined-up thinking.

* * *

One day, another girl arrived at the flat, and her name was Susan. She was as hard as nails and had the kind of face that looked like it had been chiselled from granite, but not in a good way. It soon became apparent from her pent-up anger that Susan had been brought in to protect Shafina. One afternoon, I caught them deep in conversation in the kitchen. They were discussing a neighbour who lived on the estate. Shafina had been convinced it was the same person who had caused all the recent trouble and she had asked Susan to protect her.

'You want me to go and sort them out?' the young girl asked, balling her fists together in preparation.

'Yeah,' I heard Shafina reply.

As she did so, she spotted me standing over in the kitchen doorway.

'Hi,' I said, lifting my hand in greeting.

Susan seemed a little startled and eyed me up and down, her face pulled into a sneer.

'Who's this?' she demanded to know.

She turned sharply to face Shafina.

'This is El. El, this is Susan,' Shafina said wearily, waving a quick hand between us as a makeshift introduction.

'All right …' the girl mumbled, chewing some gum in her mouth.

'So, are you and Shafina friends?' I began, trying to strike up conversation.

I had already decided that I would prefer to have Susan on my side rather than as an enemy.

She stopped chewing the gum and pushed it over to one side of her cheek using her tongue.

'S'pose you could say that. I sort people out for her, if that's what you mean.'

She folded her arms as she spoke, and I got the sense that she had a hair-trigger temper. Susan was only a year older than me, but I found her extremely intimidating. I was still racking my brains, trying to think of something else to say, when Susan said something that stopped me dead in my tracks.

'Do you know Don?'

The sheer mention of his name made my skin crawl, and I had an immediate flashback to his body lying on top of mine, his ribs crushing me as he pinned me down and raped me …

'Yeah.'

I tried to make myself busy – anything, so long as I didn't have to look at her. I opened all the kitchen cupboards, pretending to look for bread. I found some inside a bread bag, but I wasn't sure how long it had been there. Turning each slice over, I checked them for mould. When I found none, I popped two slices into the toaster. Then I began to search for butter and a knife – anything to stop me from having to look Susan in the eye.

She will know. She'll be able to tell you've had sex with him and she'll see what a silly little slag you are. I began to fret.

But she didn't. Instead, her face broke into a warm smile as she explained that Don was a friend of hers.

She doesn't have a clue.

The more she spoke about him, the more Susan seemed to thaw.

She was staring straight at me, still waiting for my reaction.

'Great!' I gushed.

I managed to muster a smile from somewhere, but I didn't mean it because I knew what he was like. Don had raped me, but what could I say?

How could I tell her? Where would I even begin?

CHAPTER THIRTEEN

RISKY BUSINESS

Despite the fact that Shafina didn't go out of the flat for long periods of time, she always seemed to know what was happening outside. I wondered if she had a spy looking out for her. Could it be Susan?

However, the more I mulled things over, the more something didn't add up about the copper who rang her every week for a friendly chat. Shafina claimed she had been the victim of domestic violence, but I'd lived at her flat for a couple of months now and I'd never once seen Blind Ash. I began to wonder if she really was a victim or if she was feeding information to the police. It seemed outlandish, but the more I thought about it, the more I began to suspect that she wasn't a victim but a police informant. No matter how many times I tried to process it, I always arrived at the same conclusion. It would certainly explain her long weekly chats with the police and how she knew what was happening – things that I certainly wasn't privy to. But then there was so much going on that I didn't know.

I didn't realise that it hadn't been a crazy dream, as Shafina had told me – my own father *had* come to the door to try to rescue me from her flat, not once but twice. I didn't realise that my parents had demanded that South Yorkshire Police rescue me from the flat of a woman who was well known in the neighbourhood for 'keeping' scantily clad girls in her flat. I didn't have a clue that Shafina's neighbours had regularly complained to South Yorkshire Police about all the dodgy comings and goings at her address – the young girls who lived there and the constant late-night visits by Asian men. I wasn't aware that her neighbours suspected Shafina of running some kind of brothel. I didn't know any of this because I'd been kept locked away from the rest of the world and from reality. My own reality was that I'd been groomed, separated from my family, and successfully detached from all I knew and loved. The grooming process had gone so deep that I believed Shafina when she told me my parents were the enemy and that she was my saviour, when she was nothing of the sort.

One morning, I woke up to find Shafina standing over me. I rubbed a hand against my eyes, and as I did, I spotted a small box in her right hand.

'I've been thinking, let's dye your hair,' she suggested, sounding quite mad.

'Whaa?' I mumbled, still trying to jump-start my brain.

'This,' she said, picking up a long strand of my waist-length dark hair between her fingers. 'Let's dye it blonde.'

Bewildered, I pushed myself up to a sitting position.

'But it's dark brown. It's always been dark brown ...' I said, yawning, as the hangover from yesterday began to kick in.

'I know, but now it's time for a change.'

I lifted both hands and massaged my head as it throbbed at my temples. As far as ideas went, this was one of her worst yet.

'No, I like my hair as it is.'

My long dark hair had always been my crowning glory and part of who I was; it was healthy and it shone in the light, just like Mel C's, my favourite Spice Girl.

'Anyway, I don't think I'll suit being blonde because ...'

'Nonsense!' Shafina snapped.

Her voice was harsh and it made me flinch.

Are you scared of her? a voice in my head questioned.

I decided I was.

Shafina was still standing there, waiting for me to agree to her latest mad plan. I realised that once she had made up her mind about something, it was almost impossible to get her to change it.

'But I've already bought it, El ... from the chemist. It was meant to be a surprise, but now you've gone and ruined it ... like you always do,' she complained in a whiny voice, sounding like a petulant child.

Shafina had one hand perched on her hip and the box of dye in the other. I eyed it nervously as she tapped her foot impatiently and her face settled into a frown. Her bottom lip protruded from her face like a wet slug, and I could tell she was gearing up for an argument. I knew better than to disagree with her because I knew she would only give me the silent treatment until life wouldn't be worth living.

'Okay. Maybe I could try ...' I mumbled.

'Great!' she said, brightening up. 'That settles it then. Get up, I'll do it now.'

With Shafina in the driving seat, I sank down on my hands and knees as she leaned over me in the bathroom. She took a deep breath and blew into a pair of clear plastic gloves to inflate them before slipping them on both hands. A strong smell of chemicals rose into the air as she mixed a couple of solutions together to form a pale-purple gloop. Using a flat brush, she began to slop the mixture all over my hair without care or attention. There was an instant chill as it covered my scalp. Soon it had warmed to an itchy tingle as the purple solution dripped down both sides of my face. I kept my eyes shut to stop the bleach from dripping into them.

'That's it, El, hold still,' Shafina said as she brushed the remainder of it onto my hair.

My nostrils flared as the acrid vapour snagged at the back of my throat. Then my scalp began to burn.

'Owww, it's hurting, Shafina!' I cried.

But she didn't want to know. Instead, she clamped a large hand firmly against my skull to hold me still so that she could apply the last scrapings.

'Shit!' she cursed.

My neck, back and chest were aching from stooping over the edge of the bath for too long; the plastic rim cut a wedge against my skin.

'What? What is it?'

Shafina huffed loudly as she picked up the packet to read something off the back.

'What is it? What's wrong?'

I was staring through half-opened eyes as the purple bleach streamed down my forehead and face, scorching everything in its path.

'Oh, nothing – I should have bought two packets, that's

all. It's your hair, it's too thick, so I've used it all up. But it says here –' she insisted, stabbing an angry finger against the box '– that there should be enough for long hair. Typical!'

In a temper, she slammed the box back down on the side.

'Oh,' I said, realising what that meant.

My hair wasn't just long, it was very long, so I realised it would be only half done and would look a bit of a state.

'Never mind, it'll be right. I'll just rub it in.'

As her fingertips burrowed against the roots of my hair, it felt as though my scalp was on fire.

'Ouch!'

I tried to scrape away some of the mixture to stop it from scorching my neckline.

'Oh, for God's sake, shut up! Stop being such a baby!'

It's all right for you, I thought bitterly. *You're not the one with a full packet of bleach plastered against your scalp!*

'Here,' she said, throwing me a threadbare, greying hand towel that had seen better days. 'Use this.'

It was the only towel in the bathroom. In fact, there was very little else inside the bathroom apart from a small bottle of cheap shampoo that was the exact same colour as green washing-up liquid. There was a small, sad patty of orange soap that had dried hard like concrete against the side of the bath. From a knee-height perspective, I noticed a grey scum line that circled the mid-way point around the bathtub. There was a collection of dead skin and oil and stray hair stuck against it – a marker of a long-forgotten soak. The more I looked, the more I saw. Strands of Shafina's thick, long black hair were curled up against the lino floor. There were more in the bottom of the bath; from a distance, they looked like fine hairline cracks in the plastic.

I wrapped the grubby towel around my head. Initially my scalp felt a little cooler, but then the towel soaked up all the heat and I started to cook beneath it. If anything, the burn and prickle of the solution seemed to intensify.

'How long do I have to keep this on?' I asked, as we wandered through to the living room.

Shafina sat smoking in her usual spot on her favourite sofa. She dipped forward, picked up her mobile phone and checked the time.

'Well, you've got dark hair and we are trying to bleach it blonde, so I reckon at least another half hour.'

Her guesstimate of time didn't exactly fill me with confidence.

Another thirty minutes of this?

Time dragged by slowly, and every so often I pushed my fingers underneath the cotton towel so I could scratch my scalp.

'Don't! Don't do that!'

I must have looked puzzled because she then added: 'It'll only make it worse – it'll irritate your skin.'

But my skin was already irritated. In fact, it felt as though it had begun to peel away, like sunburnt skin. It continued to sear over the minutes that followed. To try to kill time, Shafina smoked one cigarette after another, lighting the end of the next with the previous one. I stared over at her, trying to search out the loose strands of long black hair, but there were none. She had neatly tucked it inside her hijab. She had always worn her hijab in my company, although I had managed to see her hair on a couple of occasions. Once it had been early in the morning, just after she had woken up. The second time was when the man had scrawled graffiti over her windows.

NONCE ... PAEDOPHILE.

I was still unsure what the words meant and Shafina had refused to be drawn any further. However, I knew they were serious enough to warrant a call to the police and a brick being thrown through the window.

It must be something bad. Shafina must be someone bad.

Then there was Susan. Shafina had summoned her to pay a visit to someone on the estate; someone who Shafina had suspected of being responsible for the damage to her flat. Susan had been brought in to mete out a warning – it was obvious that whoever had been responsible for the graffiti didn't approve of Shafina or her strange lifestyle, and they had let that be known. They had even thrown a house brick through her living-room window to try to get their point across. They had wanted to give her a warning and a fright. Maybe they had wanted it to hit her – even kill her?

I gasped.

I wonder if that's why she doesn't go out very much. Maybe it's because she's hated.

'Right!' she said, giving her mobile a cursory check. 'That's you. Come on, I'll go and rinse you off.'

Obediently, I followed her through to the bathroom and knelt down at the side of the bath.

'Come on, head over,' she ordered, filling up a plastic jug with water.

My hair was dripping wet and it hung down like a curtain in front of my face as she rinsed it through. I strained my eyes to try to see what colour it was, but I was too close.

'Oh …' I heard Shafina sigh.

'What is it? What's wrong?' I panicked, my heart pounding with anxiety.

'Well, it's hardly white blonde …'

'Why? What colour is it?'

I grabbed the ends of my hair and pulled them to one side so that I could see the colour.

'Yellow!' I screeched. 'It's bright fucking yellow!'

Shafina began to snigger, which infuriated me more.

'It's not perfect, I'll give you that, and, well, I've seen better … but I'm sure it'll dry lighter. Hair always looks much darker when it's wet.'

But it wasn't funny and I wasn't buying it. I scrambled to my feet and ran into the hallway to check myself in the mirror and see how bad it actually was.

'Jesus Christ!'

I gasped, turning my head each way as I examined the limp yellow mess on my head. Running strands of hair through my hands, I tried to comb them between my fingers, but it felt like straw.

Shafina was howling with laughter. She couldn't help herself. Her laughter escaped from behind the half-opened bathroom door and travelled along the hallway.

'Come on, El,' she said, smiling as she peered around the edge of the bathroom door. 'It's not that bad!'

But it was. In fact, it was worse than bad; it was the colour of custard and felt as dry as cotton wool. My once-silken hair – my crowning glory – now felt stringy and elastic. It had been damaged and I looked almost unrecognisable.

Maybe that's what she wanted all along.

'My hair is knackered,' I remarked glumly as some of the ends snapped off in my fingers. I slumped down onto the sofa feeling utterly miserable. It looked a mess – I looked a real shambles.

Shafina glanced up from her mobile phone.

'You'll get used to it,' she remarked, not caring if I did or didn't.

But I never did.

Not long afterwards, I heard a knock at the front door. I wasn't sure where Shafina was, so I walked down the hallway and answered it. There were two women standing there on the doorstep. They smiled warmly as they greeted me, but their smiles soon faded as they took me in. Their faces seemed to cloud over with a strange look of concern as they peered inside.

'Hi,' the smaller of the two women began; her voice sounded both calm and gentle. 'Are you Elizabeth?'

I nodded and mumbled a yes as I ran a self-conscious hand through my frizzy yellow hair. My scalp was still sore and itchy, and I had to fight the urge to scratch it, even though that was all I wanted to do. I studied the women and noted that they were both wearing jeans and casual T-shirts.

They don't look like police.

'I'm Tina,' the first woman began, 'and this is my colleague Anna.'

Anna had darker hair than Tina; it was shiny and tied up in a bouncy, healthy ponytail.

That's what mine used to look like, I thought bitterly.

'We've had a referral,' Tina said, 'for you. We are youth

workers from an organisation called Risky Business, which is based right here in Rotherham … and, well, we've come to see if you're okay. Are you okay, Elizabeth?'

I nodded. As I did, I felt a presence at my side, hidden behind the half-opened door – Shafina.

'Yeah, I'm fine,' I said, trying to muster a smile.

Although, in reality, I was far from it. Instead, I felt like crying; I wanted to cut my hair off, wash, eat and claw the skin from my bones … and that was just the start. I wanted to scrub my body to rid it of the sweat and scent of the men who had raped me. I wanted to do all those things, but I couldn't say a word, not with Shafina standing there.

'Yeah, I'm fine,' I repeated.

'That's good,' Tina said as Anna nodded. It was obvious that neither believed me.

You are fooling no one. Look at the state of you!

The constant itch on my scalp ached to be scratched. It felt alive and it prickled around my ears and along the back of my neck. I couldn't stand it a moment longer – lifting my left hand, I allowed myself one small scratch. My whole body shuddered because it felt as though I had a thousand ants crawling across me and both women noticed.

'Would you like to come out with us?' the smaller one asked in a pleasant voice that didn't sound too pushy.

Shafina's hot breath brushed against my face as I tried to focus straight ahead. I didn't want to let the women know she was there, watching. Bizarrely, I didn't want to betray her.

'Nah,' I insisted, shaking my head. 'Nah, I'm good here, thanks.'

A slight flicker of disappointment brushed across Tina's face, but she soon managed to compose herself.

'Okay, that's fine, Elizabeth, but we'll come back and see you again, if that's all right?'

I shrugged my shoulders as if I didn't care either way. However, for all my bravado, I hoped that they would, because I realised that Shafina was dangerous. She was unpredictable. I suspected she had injured herself with kitchen cupboards just to get me to stay. If she had done this then there was no telling what she might do to me.

She is mad!

'Right, we'll see you again soon then,' Tina said, breaking into my thoughts.

She dipped her hand down inside a large bag and pulled out a smaller, clear plastic one.

'Before we go, we've brought this for you,' she explained, holding it out for me.

'What is it?' I asked, eyeing it suspiciously.

'Oh, it's just a few toiletries – a few bits and bobs to help you get by.'

A gift? I'd not had a gift since the mobile phone Shafina had given me.

'Right, er, thank you.'

As I took the bag from her hand, Tina smiled.

'No problem. You take care, Elizabeth.'

I smiled back at her, and the frostiness in my voice began to thaw.

'Yeah, you too.'

Then I closed the door.

Shafina was staring so intently at me that I had to turn away just to escape her gaze.

'Good girl, El.'

But instead of bringing me comfort, her words and lack of sincerity left me cold. Pushing up both sleeves, I began to scratch. I clawed at my scalp, my face and both arms until my skin was patterned with angry red welts. Then I moved onto my stomach, lower back and legs. My nails dragged against my skin, breaking it and causing it to bleed. However, my relief was short-lived as soon I began to itch all over again.

What was it? The bleach?

I glanced down at the clear, plastic bag in my hand. It contained all the things a person needed to stay clean. I realised that my arms were covered in bruises and my hands were filthy; my fingernails wcrc grimy and crusted with small, dark half-crescents of dirt, just like Hazi's had been. I shuddered as I thought of him on top of me.

That's when I realised – I hadn't washed in over two months. I hadn't washed once since moving into Shafina's flat.

CHAPTER FOURTEEN

SHAMPOO

After the women had left, Shafina wandered off into the kitchen. I saw my chance, stepped into the bathroom and closed the door. Pulling down the toilet lid, I perched myself on the end and opened up the small plastic bag. Inside were several things: shower gel, deodorant, toothpaste, toothbrush and a decent bottle of coconut shampoo.

I got to my feet and went over to the small bathroom mirror where I looked at my reflection. I wanted to see what the two women had seen when I'd answered the door to them. My hair was parched and looked a real fright; I knew, even if I used the whole bottle of shampoo, I could never hope to revive it.

Look at the state of you. You look dead behind the eyes.

I looked wan. Placing both hands against the flesh that covered my cheeks, I pulled it taut. My skin was so paper thin that my cheekbones jutted out like the edge of two knives.

You look like a junkie.

Shaking my head, I wondered how things had got this bad. As I did, the stranger in the mirror did the same. For a second her movement shocked me because I didn't recognise the girl with the brittle hair and deep, dark shadows circling two sunken eyes; her slender face and parchment skin weren't familiar to me. I didn't recognise that hollowed-out version. I lifted a curious hand and traced it along the side of my face.

'*You're beautiful* ...' Hazi's voice suddenly echoed inside my head.

I flinched as the Christina Aguilera song instantly began to play on a sick loop inside my head. I pulled away my hand sharply. Clamping both eyes shut, I tried to block out the song, his voice and his face as it zoomed into view.

'No,' I whispered. Up until this moment, I'd seen no point in washing myself, my self-esteem was so low. Subconsciously, I think I had been trying to make myself less attractive, so that the men would leave me alone.

I pushed Hazi's image from my mind, but his face was replaced with Don's. I struggled to breathe as I felt his weight on top of me, his expensive aftershave, the smell of male sweat as he pulled down my clothes and began to rape me ...

My eyes opened wide with fear as my heart hammered.

Breathe, remember to breathe ...

I couldn't do this, not anymore; I had to get out.

I held the bottle of shampoo in my hand. It was only a bottle – the type you could pick up in any supermarket – but it was a good brand. The kindness of the women had made me want to weep. The iridescent bottle caught the light as I turned it over and over in my hands; it wasn't cheap and nasty, like the one Shafina kept in the bathroom. It was like the one Mum bought and it reminded me of home.

Almost immediately, I had different men calling me at different times of the day and night, all pestering me to meet and have sex. And I did. I had sex with them all – apart from one. It sounds strange, I know, but I was damaged beyond belief and any attention felt good right then. It made me feel as though I belonged to something and I convinced myself these men cared for me. They weren't much, but they were all I had. They would abuse me in the backs of cars or at a rented house near the centre of Rotherham. Each man would drive me over to the house – a small, two-bedroom terrace – where they would pin me down and rape me. The house was a bit run-down and the front garden was small, overgrown and shabby. It stood out like a sore thumb against the other, smarter family houses that lined the rest of the street. From the outside the property seemed neglected, and it wasn't much better inside. The house was empty apart from three heavily patterned black sofas that had been pushed up against a wall inside the cramped living room. Even one sofa would have been too much, but three gave it an overwhelming sense of claustrophobia. The property seemed totally unloved and unlived in, and it later transpired that the men rented it so that they had a base to take young girls for illegal sex. The magnolia walls were all scuffed and the plain yellow curtains were grubby, but they served their purpose in keeping out the prying eyes of the world. Upstairs, there were two small bedrooms, with beds, and I had sex in them both. The bathroom was plain and empty; it had nothing – no soap or even a towel – to wash with. Ironically, the house was an empty shell, just like me. I didn't tell anyone what was happening, although Tina at Risky Business eventually found out and told me to stay away from the men, but I couldn't. By now, I was caught in the middle of a vicious circle – it was just my way of life.

When we weren't over at the house, the men would take me up to the top field in Clifton Park for sex. The area was pretty deserted and surrounded by trees, so it suited them well. The gang would ply me with Smirnoff vodka and cola until my legs grew unsteady, which made me much easier to manage. I'm ashamed to admit that it was all I felt I was worth – to be the sexual plaything of these animals.

Not all of the men wanted sex. One man in particular was extremely arrogant and looked down his nose at me, but the other seven saw me as a body to use and abuse. I didn't realise it then, but the gang was doing the exact same thing to a number of other vulnerable young girls.

I lived at the children's home by choice for almost a year, with regular contact twice a week with Mum and Dad, before it was decided that I had to leave. To be fair to the staff, they had tried their hardest, but my behaviour was at best unpredictable and at worse volatile. In short, I was a damaged child who was displaying signs of distress. Tragically, I'd convinced myself I was in charge of my life and was making my own decisions, when the reality was that these men were doing that for me. I was being used and exploited again, but if I thought things were bad then, I was wrong, because things were about to get so much worse.

CHAPTER SEVENTEEN

HOSTEL

I was around sixteen and a half when the authorities decided to move me again, this time to another hostel for my own safety. The others hadn't been able to control me or hem me in, and now I was sixteen I was seen as an adult. Ironically, the hostel was even closer to Clifton Park – the place my abusers congregated – than the children's home. Unwittingly, they had just made the sexual exploitation of me so much easier. The hostel was a real down-at-heel type of place made up of two houses. One was for young adults who were classed as semi-independent, while the other was to house those who were deemed to be independent. I'd never lived on my own, so I moved into the first house. Initially, I shared a bedroom with a girl called Amber, who was really strange. Amber didn't mix with the other residents. Instead, she was paranoid and would 'report' each and every one of us to the staff. Unsurprisingly, our living arrangements didn't last very long and soon I was given another room in the other 'independent' block. Once there, I became good friends with a lad called Tim and soon he had become like a brother to me. Tall and really skinny, Tim became my best friend, but he had a really sad backstory. He had grown up in different care homes because his parents had never wanted him. As a result, Tim had become involved with drugs, yet unlike others I knew who did drugs, Tim didn't have a selfish bone in his body. Instead, he would constantly look out for me and make sure that I ate properly. We would often share the food Mum and Dad brought in for me. Back then, I received Jobseeker's Allowance, which was £140 every fortnight. However, I'd blow the lot on vodka and drugs, as by now I was regularly taking ecstasy pills and amphetamines, so Tim would cook for me and feed me. I hadn't been living there very long when he broached the subject of all the random Pakistani men he'd seen me hanging around with.

'They don't give a shit about you, El,' Tim insisted.

We were sitting, smoking a cigarette in my bedsit when he spoke to me. At first, I didn't have a clue what he was talking about.

'Who doesn't?'

He took a drag of his cigarette.

'Those Pakistani men. I've seen them, picking you up all times of the day and night, but I'm telling you, El, they're using you. They don't care about you.'

I hated people telling me what to do, but with Tim I decided to make an exception because we were living in the same hostel and his earlier life had been fucked up too, just like mine had. I trusted his advice because he'd also been abused, only in a different way. I knew Tim was genuine and he wanted the best for me.

'They're all right. They give me stuff ... alcohol and fags,' I said, trying to justify it both to him and myself.

He pulled a face as though I was crackers.

'It doesn't matter; it's not worth it, El. Whatever they give you, please don't hang around with them. They're bad news. Keep away from them – they're no good for you.'

I stifled a chuckle because I knew that he meant well and was trying to protect me, but I'd already decided that I could and would look after myself. In some small way, I also believed it to be 'normal'.

'They're my friends,' I insisted.

I just couldn't accept that I wasn't in control of my life and never had been. It was just another lie I told to stop myself from going under.

Although I was a difficult and damaged child, Yvonne, the woman from the local authority, decided that my behaviour was all down to the fact that I was 'naughty'. She contacted Mum and told her to cut off everything, including the treats and my shopping. She told my parents this would encourage me to 'behave' because I was still being groomed and seeing these men. There wasn't much they could do about it because, ashamed, I was secretive and tried to cut myself off from them, but thankfully they didn't listen to Yvonne or to me. They realised that the officials who were supposedly there to protect me had done anything but. It was just another example of how young girls like me were being routinely failed by the authorities. Only my parents and the youth workers at Risky Business seemed to have my best interests at heart.

* * *

Drug-taking was commonplace among the hostel residents, and the drug of choice seemed to be ecstasy. The first time I tried it, I felt amazing. I also knew that, with Tim there to watch over me, I would never come to any harm, and I didn't. We would walk into Rotherham together to visit a group of Pakistani men who we knew were drug dealers. They would sell us five ecstasy pills for a tenner, which was really cheap, even back then. I'm not sure what the pills had been cut with, but they seemed to work and I seemed to be off my face more often than not. On the occasions when we couldn't get hold of ecstasy, we would replace it with amphetamines. One day, all the residents in our block – seven in total – decided to take amphetamines for seven days straight. It was utter madness and it almost drove me to the brink. We were so off our faces that we decided to go to Clifton Park in the middle of the night. I was so far gone that I began to hallucinate and spotted fairies hanging from the tree branches. When I later told Tim, he pissed himself laughing. We all did.

But the following weekend something serious happened that would sober us all up. When I returned in the evening to the hostel I was greeted by all the residents pacing around outside. They seemed extremely anxious, and I heard a girl called Kate screaming over in the corner. It was clear that she was in some kind of distress. I scanned the faces, looking for Tim. I wandered over and tapped him on the arm.

'What the hell has happened? What's wrong with everyone?'

He turned and I could tell immediately from the look on his face that whatever it was, it was something really bad. He seemed to be utterly devastated.

'It's David,' he said, his voice catching in the back of his throat.

'What is it? What's wrong with him?'

Tim glanced over at Kate, who was being comforted by the rest of the group. David was her boyfriend.

'It's horrible, El. Something terrible has happened,' he said, pulling me over to one side.

'What? Just tell me.'

His reaction was beginning to scare me. I'd never seen Tim like this. He ran an anxious hand through his hair and as he did I realised that his whole body was trembling.

'Just tell me!'

Tim's eyes met mine.

'They had a row, Kate and David. I don't know what it was about, but it was a bad one ...' he began.

I nodded to try to hurry the rest of the story out of him.

'Anyway, he stormed off, but no one knew where he'd gone. We all thought he'd just come back later when he'd calmed down, only he didn't.'

'Why? Where is he? What's happened to him?'

'Well, that's it, you see. He was found on his own nearby ... El –' he said, beginning to shake uncontrollably, 'David ... well, he tried to kill himself.'

I gasped in horror.

'I told you it was horrible.'

I glanced all around; everyone was crying. Lots of people were crowded around Kate, trying to comfort her, but it was obvious that she was beyond distress.

'Is he ... is he ... alive?'

Tim nodded. 'Yeah, but only just. He's at the hospital now.'

Of course, Kate was completely heartbroken, but as the days passed the news from the hospital grew a little more hopeful. Somehow, David had survived, but overnight the incident seemed to change the mood of the entire block. For the first time, I appreciated just how fleeting life could be, including my own. It should have made me more careful, but it seemed to have the opposite effect.

One day, after a particularly heavy night on drugs, Pat, the manager of the hostel, came into my bedsit and lifted up the duvet. The cold air settled against my warm skin, rousing me.

'W-w-what you doing?' I groaned, still half unconscious.

'I'm checking you're alive – that's what I'm doing!'

Pat was in her forties and had a daughter the exact same age as me. 'That's why I care,' she'd insisted, time and time again.

Yet in spite of her best efforts, and the fact that she wouldn't let anyone over the doorstep, I tried to destroy her faith in me, and it wasn't long before I tested even Pat's patience to its limit.

CHAPTER EIGHTEEN

TAKEN

One day, a man called Khaan – someone I'd never met before in my life – texted to ask if I would meet him and his friend. I was with a girl called Jade so I told her I'd agreed to meet them and would have to leave.

Jade looked over.

'I could come with you?' she offered.

'Okay.'

It was around 2 p.m. when we met Khaan on the corner of a nearby street. He pulled up in a large, knackered black car. Sitting next to him in the passenger seat was his friend Chamali, or Cham for short. Both men seemed really friendly, but then I was so conditioned to do exactly what I was told that when they asked us to climb into the back seat, I did, and Jade followed.

The men were young, and both wore Nike tracksuits with matching trainers, which I thought was a bit naff. In spite of their flashy clothes, Khaan's car was a real old banger – it looked as though it was held together with sticky tape. As we climbed in and slammed the back doors, Khaan pushed his foot down hard on the accelerator and the exhaust roared as we took off at high speed.

'Here, Cham, pass the girls some beer, will you?' Khaan said.

His mate dipped down and pulled out some bottles from a plastic bag down in the footwell.

Jade turned to me and grinned as though we had just won the lottery. I smiled but I felt uneasy. I couldn't put my finger on it, but something felt distinctly off about these men.

The inside of the car smelled of cheap aftershave and of two young men trying much too hard to impress. As the streets of Rotherham whirred by in a blur outside, the uncomfortable silence was broken by a loud hiss as Cham pulled off the bottle tops with an opener. He passed a beer to Jade and handed another to me.

'Thanks,' Jade said, taking it from him.

She turned towards me so that we could chink our bottles together. The glass clattered loudly, making Cham laugh.

'I've also got vodka and lemonade in here, girls,' he said, waving a large plastic pop bottle in the air.

Cham unscrewed the top, took a long swig and handed it to Khaan. He was driving but he took a gulp all the same. As he passed the bottle back to Cham, the two men looked at each other conspiratorially. My stomach clenched with uncertainty, but I didn't want to ruin the day out for Jade so I sipped my beer and tried to quell the rising sense of unease.

Soon, we had reached the outskirts of Rotherham and, according to the road signs, we seemed to be heading over towards the M1 motorway.

'Khaan, where are we going?' I asked, sitting up in my seat.

His tracksuit rustled as he twisted in the driver's seat to look back at me.

'Call me Kai. That's what my mates call me.'

I nodded but my mind was distracted as Rotherham began to quickly disappear behind us.

'Okay. Where are we going … Kai?'

There was a pause as he pulled out a cigarette and lit it. He inhaled the smoke slowly as though considering what to say next.

'Somewhere different. You'll see. We're going for a drive, that's all,' he said, pressing the play button on his car CD player.

Kai's eyes darted over towards Cham, who cranked up the volume to drown out any more questions I might have. Loud dance music bounced off the walls and doors as the tinny car pulsated with a deafening bassline. I watched as the grey fabric roof above my head vibrated in time to the music.

THUD, THUD, THUD.

I'd expected Kai and Cham to take us to Clifton Park or somewhere else in Rotherham, but we were heading away from town at speed. Moments later, we took a slip road off the roundabout, Kai indicated right and we joined the M1 motorway. My eyes scanned the layby, searching for a blue sign to tell me which way we were heading. One whizzed by and I had to twist my head quickly to try to read it. We were travelling south. I gulped my beer anxiously as I tried to work out what the hell to do.

You need to get out of this car NOW!

Anxiety overwhelmed me – my heart hammered inside my chest as the palms of my hands prickled with a nervous sweat.

'You girls want some pills?' Kai asked.

Cham held out his hand. In the centre of his palm were two pale-pink pills, which I guessed might be ecstasy.

Jade's face lit up.

'Nah, we're fine, thanks,' I said quickly, answering for both of us.

Her face crumpled with disappointment and Cham noticed.

'Er, I think your mate wants to try one. Don't you?' he insisted, holding his hand out to Jade. 'Go on, take these pills, they're good stuff.'

I continued to refuse for both of us because I had a gut feeling that these men were bad news, but Cham wouldn't take no for an answer.

'You might as well take them because we've got drop-offs …' Kai said, butting in.

Drop-offs? Are these guys proper drug dealers?

My body was facing forward but I stole a quick side-glance at Jade. She saw me shake my head ever so slightly, urging her not to take the pill, although I knew she was really tempted.

'What are they?' she said, asking Cham.

He grinned.

These men are dangerous.

My senses were on full alert. I couldn't explain why, I just knew Kai and his mate were dodgy. Other men had used and abused me over the years, but there was something really sinister about these two. They carried themselves with an air of arrogance and they seemed in a whole different league – a much more dangerous one – to the other Pakistani men I knew.

'They're good shit, man,' Cham said, trying to encourage Jade.

I glared at her to leave it and, thankfully, she did. With no takers for his pills, Cham huffed and turned back in his seat. I stared out of the windscreen and along the motorway as the car seemed to swallow it up, mile by mile.

'You're missing out, y'know?' Cham added with a shrug of his shoulders.

He was refusing to let the matter go, which made me even more suspicious.

'Can we turn the music down a bit?' I begged.

'Why?'

'Because I've got a banging headache.'

Cham leaned forward, twisted a button and the volume faded.

With him still facing towards the road, I secretly slid my right hand inside the pocket of my trackie top and pulled out my mobile. Jade was busy staring out of the other passenger window, so I scrolled through my contacts, found Tina's number and pressed the call button. The phone rang for a moment and then the display changed, indicating that she had answered. But instead of picking up my phone and chatting to her, I left the line open so that she could listen in to our conversation.

'Where are you taking me and Jade again?' I asked, loudly enough for Tina to hear.

Kai snorted with laughter.

'What are you, deaf or something? I told you, we're taking you for a drive.'

'Yeah,' I replied, this time with much more confidence than I actually felt. 'I know that, but we're on the M1 and now we're leaving South Yorkshire and heading towards Derby …'

I knew this for a fact because I'd just spotted another blue mileage sign at the side of the road.

Kai shook his head as though I was a bit thick, but Cham turned in his seat so that he was facing me. I was sitting in the seat directly behind him, so he didn't see the mobile phone nestling in the centre of my lap.

'Come on, girls, take these pills. They'll make you chill. Make you feel really good, you know what I'm saying?'

Jade laughed and her resolve seemed to crumble – she dipped forward to look again as the car charged along the motorway. Kai indicated and the vehicle moved over to the outside lane at high speed.

'Don't, Jade. Please don't take those pills. You don't know what's in them,' I begged.

Cham's eyes switched over to me and he seemed angry, as though he was offended.

'What do you mean? I wouldn't give you no bad shit. These are good shit, man. Aren't they, boy?' he said, directing his question towards Kai.

'Yeah, just take 'em. They'll make you feel reaaaal niiiice …' he replied, stretching out the words.

I shivered with fear – we were trapped in a fast-moving car with two strange men, travelling God only knew where.

Those pills could be anything, I wanted to scream out loud, but I didn't dare.

Jade shifted in her seat as she leaned in towards me.

'Come on, El, it'll be fun – it'll be a laugh!'

'That's it!' Cham said, encouraging her. 'Don't be

boring, like her – try 'em. You'll never know until you do.'

Spurred on by Cham, Jade plucked one of the pills from his hand and held it up towards her lips.

'Don't take it, Jade. You don't know what's in them – they could be cut with anythin—'

But it was too late. I watched in horror as she popped the tablet on the tip of her tongue and closed her mouth.

'Jade, please don't!'

Her throat contracted once and then twice as she swallowed the pill down with a glug of beer.

'That's my girl,' Cham said, nudging Kai.

'Now, where's that vodka?' Jade said, beginning to giggle.

My stomach fell away, as though I was sitting on an out-of-control fairground dipper. Jade had just taken something – God only knew what – and now it was up to me to get us both out of there. Panic gripped me as I gulped air like water.

I desperately hoped that Tina could hear everything that was being said. I decided to keep talking. At least that way I could give her a running commentary of where we were and what was happening. However, the further we travelled, the more I began to wonder how she could help. Surreptitiously, I checked the battery on my phone. It was almost full, and I was thankful that I'd remembered to charge it earlier that morning. But now it was the afternoon and the light outside was beginning to fade. The watery autumn sun had dipped down and was disappearing from the horizon. I prayed that my phone battery would hold out long enough for us to reach wherever the men had planned to take us.

After forty minutes, the tablet Jade had swallowed began to take effect. She suddenly became hyper and started to laugh like a maniac. Soon she was talking ten to the dozen, although she wasn't making much sense.

'Are we there yet?' she asked Kai, shaking him by the shoulder.

'Nah, but we're not far.'

But Jade wouldn't leave it.

'Are we there yet …? Are we there yet …? Are we there yet …?' she asked over and over.

Kai grew annoyed and told her to be quiet, but Cham just laughed. It was the drugs – whatever that pill had been – that was doing this to her, but I was also frightened. We wouldn't stand a cat in hell's chance of escape if she was like this.

'I'm floating … I'm floating,' she laughed, as though lost in another world.

What the hell was in those pills?

In a panic, I continued to read signs out loud so that Tina would know exactly where we were.

'Christ, you are a crazy pair of white bitches …' Cham said, shaking his head in despair.

'Are we there yet …? Are we there yet …?' Jade piped up again.

Kai grew annoyed and slapped the steering wheel hard with the palm of his hand.

'Fuck's sake! Shut up, will you?'

But Cham was pissing himself laughing.

I could tell that things might turn ugly, so I took Jade's hand in mine and gave it a reassuring squeeze.

'It's okay, I'm here.'

I was desperately trying to quieten her down, and even though she was getting on my nerves, I knew I couldn't abandon her. We had to escape, and we had to do it together.

I suspected she had swallowed some ecstasy, but I also knew that eventually it would wear off. I just hoped this would happen before we reached our destination, wherever that was. Leaning over, I opened Jade's window slightly and hoped that the cool air might help bring her round. I'd been drinking beer, but with fear and adrenalin coursing through my veins I felt completely sober. My eyes drifted over to the speedometer. Kai was doing over 90 mph. I twisted, found my seatbelt and clicked it on before doing the same to Jade. Up until that point, neither of us had thought about putting them on.

A short while later, Kai indicated and we pulled off the M1 onto the A42, heading towards Birmingham.

'Why are we taking the A42 to Birmingham?' I asked in a loud voice.

Please let Tina hear this …

I glanced down at the mobile in my lap to check that she was still connected. She was.

'Chill, El, I told you, we're taking you somewhere nice,' Kai leered.

'What? Birmingham? Are you taking us to Birmingham?'

He refused to answer. Instead, his eyes shifted sideways to Cham, who turned and offered me another beer.

I waved a hand in front of my face.

'No, thanks. I've had enough.'

My refusal made Cham snigger.

'But you've only had one, and you wouldn't take those

pills. What is she, boy?' he said, looking over at Kai to join in the piss-take. 'Is she a nun or summat?'

'Yeah, I reckon so.' Kai grinned and then both men broke into laughter.

I ignored them and held Jade's hand in mine. It felt warm and, for once, she'd stopped talking. In fact, she had grown unnervingly quiet. We needed to get help, and fast.

The car sped along the motorway skirting around Birmingham before heading back towards the M1. We stayed on the M1 for what seemed like ages, until Kai finally indicated and we pulled off again, this time onto a road towards central London.

'Are we going to London? I asked, desperate to give Tina some idea of where in the country we were.

We had been in the car for well over two hours and I had no clue where we were heading or what these men planned to do with us. My anxiety tightened like a balled fist and rested heavily in the pit of my stomach.

What the hell are they going to do to us?

London. I'd never been to London, but I imagined that two teenage girls like us would be swallowed up inside a city as big as that. Two daft girls from Yorkshire, two country bumpkins.

We wouldn't stand a chance.

For years, I'd been a child playing adult games, only now things had gone too far. We were trapped inside this car, travelling far too fast, heading – where?

Kai clicked the indicator upwards.

'London!' I announced again, hoping Tina was still on the other end of the line and that she could hear. 'You're taking us to central London!'

'Yeah!' Kai said, punching the air triumphantly.

Jade was still really quiet.

'Jade … Jade … are you okay?' I asked, shaking her by the arm to try to rouse her.

Thankfully, the young girl grumbled and rubbed her eyes before opening them. She took in her surroundings, but she seemed confused and a little startled.

'We're in London. They've brought us to London …' I explained, hoping it would calm her.

Suddenly, the car drove into the outskirts of the city. With every street sign that passed, I began to read aloud so that Tina could follow our route and try to locate us. The more Jade seemed to come down from her high, the more frightened she became. She sat up in her seat and glanced around anxiously. The skin on her face was creased where she'd been leaning against the seatbelt.

She pulled a sleeve over her hand and used it to wipe some of the condensation off the passenger window.

'Why are we in London, El?'

I didn't know what to tell her because I had no idea.

The car slowed as we pulled into what looked like an industrial estate.

Christ! What are they planning to do to us?

'Why have you brought us here? What are you …?' However, just as I'd begun to ask them, both men glanced at each other, pulled open their car doors and legged it into the night.

Jade looked at me in horror as a cool breeze drifted in through the two open doors.

'What the fuck?'

I turned and peered through the back window. It was pitch black outside, but the men had scarpered. Now we were all alone. Suddenly, the whole situation felt extremely ominous.

Is someone waiting for us?

'Tina,' I said, lifting the mobile to my ear. 'I don't know where we are, but they've gone. The men have gone. They've left us in some industrial estate in London …'

Jade looked at me in confusion. 'Who are you talking to?'

I shook my head and grabbed the door handle, indicating for her to do the same.

'It doesn't matter – let's just get out of here … fast! Come on!'

Jade grabbed the handle on her side and we both legged it away from the car into the shadows. My heart was beating so fast that I found it difficult to try to catch my breath.

Is someone here waiting to grab us? Are we being watched?

My feet slipped and stumbled against broken concrete as we searched for somewhere to hide.

'What can you see, El?'

It was Tina.

'There's a sign,' I replied, reading it out loud.

Tina repeated it to someone else in the office so that they could search for an address online.

'El, listen to me. What else can you see?'

I glanced all around, trying to pick out shapes in the darkness.

'Bins. I can see some large bins over in the corner.'

'Right,' Tina said, speaking slowly and clearly. 'I want you both to hide behind those bins – and, El?'

'Yes.'

'This is really important: do NOT come out until I tell you it is safe to do so. Do you understand?'

'Yes.'

'Good. Now do it!'

I turned to Jade. 'We need to hide behind those bins over there,' I whispered, gesturing over to them. 'Follow me.'

Panting for breath, Jade and I sprinted over towards the bins and crouched down behind them.

'Now, can you see them? Can you see the men?' Tina said.

My eyes searched through the gloom. 'No.'

'Good. Now, wait there. Jayne is on the phone to the police right now.'

Jayne Senior was a manager who worked at Risky Business. Like Tina, Jayne was kind and she really cared about all the kids they dealt with.

'Tina, we are in the middle of nowhere. Everything looks shut,' I whispered, trying to keep my voice low.

'It doesn't matter – we think we know where you are, and we are trying to get help right now.'

Unbeknown to me, Jayne had rung the local police and then South Yorkshire Police, but neither force wanted to get involved.

Suddenly, I felt a hand grab the top of my arm and I almost jumped out of my skin in fright. I expected to find Cham or Kai standing there, but it was Jade.

'Who is it? Who are you talking to?'

'Tina – she's from Risky Business. It's okay, she's sound. She'll help us,' I insisted.

Tina was still waiting on the other end of the phone.

'El, are you both okay?'

'Yeah, we're fine. Jade took a pill, but you're fine now, aren't you?' I asked, pushing some hair away from her eyes.

Jade nodded.

'And you, El?'

'I'm fine – I didn't take anything. I just didn't trust them, Tina, they were well dodgy …'

'I know. I heard you. I was listening in the whole time. You did really well, El. Now, I just need you both to keep calm and stay hidden until we can get someone to come and help you. Jayne's working on it right now.'

My eyes darted all around but there didn't seem to be a soul in sight. Through the gloom I spotted something – the pale-yellow glow of a lamp inside a Portakabin.

'Hang on, I can see a light. There's someone in there.'

A few seconds passed, then the Portakabin door swung open and a man holding a torch appeared. The beam of light flashed over towards the empty car – which now had all four doors open – and then over at us. It was a security man; I could tell by his black uniform.

'Tina, someone's coming!' I said, beginning to panic.

'It's okay, El. Go and speak to him. Jayne has told him you're there. He's going to help you.'

'Really?'

'Yes. It's okay, she's explained everything.'

As we'd stayed hidden behind the bins, Jayne had spoken to the security guard and told him that two vulnerable girls had been abducted and abandoned inside the yard. With the police unwilling to help, the guard had offered to come and find us and keep an eye on us until Risky Business managed to sort something out. He invited us to sit in a waiting room with him so that we could keep warm.

'Are you hungry? Is there anything you need?' he asked us.

'No, but thanks,' I replied.

The guard, who had grandchildren our age, was beyond kind.

Jade was shell-shocked and stared straight ahead. She was completely freaked out by what might have been.

An hour or so later, two officers from the local police arrived to pick us up, but they didn't ask us anything; in truth, they couldn't wait to get shot of us. One of the officers called the police in South Yorkshire, who refused to come and pick us up. I could hear them bickering over the phone about whose responsibility we were. Although I had Kai's mobile number, no one seemed interested in it or the abandoned car. They just wanted us to go home so they didn't have to deal with it. In the end, Risky Business went halves with our hostel and paid for two train tickets home so that we could return safely. We finally pulled into Rotherham station around 11 p.m. – over nine hours after we'd left Rotherham.

Of course, Pat had been fully briefed on what had happened and was sick with worry about us both.

'You can't keep doing this, El. You're not only putting yourself in danger, but Jade too.'

I was knackered and I couldn't be bothered to argue. Instead, I just shrugged her off.

My view is that the men had taken us to London for a sinister reason, and although there was no way to prove it, I believe we'd been part of a wider drugs deal. I think the men had taken us there so that we could be traded as sex slaves.

If the staff at Risky Business hadn't been on the other end of the line, I honestly do not think Jade and I would still be alive today.

CHAPTER NINETEEN

THE GUN

I'd been living at the hostel for almost a year when there was another serious incident. One evening, a member of staff was enjoying a cigarette outside when a car containing two British-Pakistani men pulled up. As usual, I was out for the evening and so wasn't around. I had been desperately trying to widen my circle of friends, but the grooming gangs always seemed to be there, connected in some way. It was, it seemed, a very small world.

'Is El Harper here?' the driver of the car demanded to know as he pulled up.

The staff member told him that she wasn't allowed to confirm or deny if I even lived there. In a temper, the man became aggressive and produced a gun. He held it up in the air and pointed it out of the car window as though he intended to use it. The member of staff was absolutely terrified. In a panic, she ran back inside the hostel and rang the police to report it as the men drove off, laughing, into the night. By the time I'd returned later that evening, all hell had broken loose. I'd been off my face with some 'friends' on ecstasy pills and was only just starting to come around.

'El, I need a word,' Pat said, calling me over as I stumbled in through the door.

'Yeah, later …' I said, wafting my hand in her face.

I couldn't even be bothered to have a conversation. The truth was, I didn't care about myself or anyone else for that matter. But Pat did. She'd put her trust in me since day one, and now even she had reached the end of the road. She knew that I couldn't carry on like this.

'I'm sorry, El, but you have to leave,' Pat insisted, looking me straight in the eye.

I swayed slightly with the after-effects of the drugs and alcohol.

'Whaaa? Why?' I mumbled, utterly confused.

She began to explain all about the men, the gun and how they'd pulled it out and threatened a member of staff.

'The thing is, El, I've given you countless chances and I'm willing to give you countless more. However, I cannot have my staff and the other young people here put at risk because of you, your behaviour and the company you keep.'

'Yeah, but –'

She held up her hand to stop me. I was seventeen and thought I knew it all, but Pat had been manager of the hostel for years, so she had seen it all.

'I'm sorry, El, but that's how it is. I've a duty of care to my staff and the other residents here.'

The ecstasy and booze quickly began to wear off. Pat's words and her frankness had sobered me up. Although I didn't want to leave the hostel because I'd made good friends there, I understood where she was coming from. Elizabeth Harper was bad news; she brought nothing but trouble to the doorstep. It was what I did and what I'd become. I realised that Pat hadn't taken the decision lightly because she had always been so totally supportive. She also cared about every single young person there, so, as manager, she was responsible for us all, not just me.

'It's okay, Pat. I understand.'

'I'm sorry, El. It's just, you've left me with no choice.'

She was right, I hadn't.

Pat's face crumpled with exhaustion. She'd had enough and I understood why. Since moving to the hostel, ecstasy and booze had become the main staples of my life. The only other constant had been sex with random Pakistani men in parks, cars and a dodgy terraced house. The original group of eight had expanded until I was having sex with up to twenty men at any one time. The hostel had put up with it all, but now Pat had had enough. I'd grown from being an abused and traumatised child into a pissed-up lunatic; I was so numb that I felt like nothing or no one could hurt me. Nothing could touch me because I'd lost all sense of normality. In short, my life had become a car crash.

'Honestly, Pat, it's fine,' I replied.

She didn't have to explain further because I understood.

The men I'd become involved with had become a threat to other people's safety. Over the course of a year, I'd brought all that and more to the hostel's front door. Unbeknown to me, Pat had been taking regular notes of car registration plates and keeping a log of all the comings and goings of me and the other children under her charge. Pat was conscientious and had been keeping an eye on all of us, but particularly me. At one point, my personal file had become so full, bulging with descriptions of the men and their cars, that Pat had to lock it away. The information was sensitive because it held the key to all my abusers. Pat had realised this and had reported the men time and time again, but the police didn't seem to want to know. South Yorkshire Police had failed to act upon her concerns or information, deciding that, now I was seventeen, almost eighteen, it was how I'd chosen to live my life. But the truth was I was still very much a child, and a vulnerable one at that.

Within the month, I was moved again. Before I left, I went to find Tim to tell him I was being kicked out. His first reaction was to laugh.

'Why are you laughing?' I asked, a little baffled.

'Because it's funny.'

Tim was laughing so hard that I found myself joining in. Both of us were wetting ourselves so much that we had tears streaming down our faces. It's hard to explain, but laughter is one of the best defence mechanisms, especially for a child. I completely understood why Tim found it so funny because I'd experienced the exact same thing with other children who had grown up in care. It was much easier for them to detach themselves from people and their own emotions, rather than face up to them. By building a wall so that they didn't become too attached, they could survive a lifestyle of constant shift and change. From a relatively young age, Tim had been abandoned by his parents, and now, like everyone else in his life, I was leaving too.

'I'll keep in touch – we can still meet up,' I promised.

'Yeah,' he mumbled as though he didn't believe a word of it.

But I proved Tim wrong, and we did keep in touch over the years that followed. So, one day, when I received a phone call from a mutual friend to say that Tim had been stabbed in a street in Sheffield, I prepared to dash to hospital to be by his side.

'He's dead, El. He didn't make it.'

Tim was just thirty-one years old. That day, my heart broke for my friend and all the other kids like him – the ones who didn't make it through. Hooked on drink and drugs from an early age, Tim had spent the rest of his life addicted. He didn't stand a chance – although it wasn't the drugs that killed him in the end but a drug debt. A debt he had paid for with his life.

After I'd been kicked out by Pat, I moved to another hostel, made up of twenty bedsits. There were three separate blocks in total; my block was separated into eight different bedsits, and unlike the previous place, this hostel was full of adult men and women, most of whom were fully blown heroin addicts. Given my past, I was now an addict too – only I was hooked on amphetamines, ecstasy tablets and booze.

It wasn't long before I met a girl there called Lisa, who was seventeen – the same age as me. Unlike the other residents, Lisa and I were still kids, so we bonded. Tragically, we had both been abused by the same grooming gangs. There was an older guy who lived there called Derek. There was something distinctly odd about him. He liked to spend his days hanging around by the main entrance. Derek would always say hello and try to engage me and Lisa in conversation, but we ignored him because he gave us the creeps. He would sneak around, watching everyone. Looking back, he obviously had mental health problems. The irony was we actually would have been much safer with Derek than we were in the company we were keeping. Other than Derek and the security guard, we never saw another soul. This meant the hostel was eerily quiet. At first, I presumed it was because the other residents kept themselves to themselves. Then I realised that everyone was just off their heads behind closed doors.

Although I only stayed at that hostel a short while, I do not know how I didn't end up a heroin addict myself, because I was surrounded by it there. Bizarrely, I didn't see myself as having a drug problem, although in reality I was exactly like them, because I used drugs to get through each day too. The only differences were that I used other drugs and these people were older than me.

For the first time since I'd left Shafina's flat, I felt utterly vulnerable again. At least at the last place I'd always had Pat to watch my back. Although there was a security guard on the front door, the hostel was a free-for-all. The security guard would ask people to sign in, but the men visiting me just used fake names so they didn't leave a paper trail. In short, because I was almost eighteen, no one seemed to care what I did or who I saw, apart from Mum and Dad. They would call by once a week, bearing bags of shopping to try to help me out. In truth, they just wanted me back home, but I felt far too feral to inflict myself upon them.

How can you ever be normal again?

Selfishly, a large part of me also didn't want to give up my 'lifestyle' – whatever that was. But it wasn't a 'lifestyle'; in truth, I was just about surviving. I was addicted, and addiction made me selfish. All I ever thought about was where I would get my next fix – drugs or booze. I'd anaesthetise myself with both to try to blunt my emotions. As long as I did that, I could almost convince myself that I was having fun.

Now I was in my own place, random groups of Pakistani men would come and go as they pleased. They would knock at the door at all different times of the night and early morning. My bedsit was situated on the ground floor, and often I'd be asleep in bed when someone would open the window and just climb through. Soon, one visitor turned into five men – all strangers to me who had been introduced to the group by other members. They would arrive clutching dope and bottles of vodka in return for sex; all of them smoked spliffs and they all drank, even though they were supposedly Muslim. There was something else too; the men who now called to see me were younger. Unlike Don and Hazi, who had been almost double my age, these men were in their early twenties. Bizarrely, the older I got, the younger my abusers became. For once, the men were only six or seven years older than me, rather than decades. Together, we would get pissed and stoned while listening to bassline niche – a kind of dance music that had originated in the clubs of Sheffield. At the time, I saw them as friends, rather than abusers.

There was a TV set in my bedsit, but I never watched it. There was also a fridge and Mum would fill it with food that I never bothered to eat. I didn't have a proper diet and I would either binge eat or starve myself. It was the only thing I had any control over.

Lisa and I would spend our days hanging around the town centre. There was also a pub – just down the road from the hostel – where underage drinking was positively encouraged. We would go and allow our Pakistani friends to buy us drinks. They did, but only so that we became more amenable to their constant demands for sex. Back at my bedsit, I would be either too drunk or drugged to stop them. One by one they would take it in turns to pin me down and rape me. Some of the men would use condoms, but many didn't. Their faces blurred into one, until soon my flat became 'party central'. Now, instead of hanging around Clifton Park, the men would congregate inside my room. Something had to give – and, finally, it did.

I had started to loathe my life, but not as much as I did myself. I couldn't carry on like this, otherwise I would either end up dead in my bedsit or my body would be found dumped in a ditch. I knew I had to make a change and somehow had to try to make it stop, but weirdly, fate intervened. In spite of all the weight I'd lost back at Shafina's flat, my body continued to develop. My hips widened and my breasts filled out; I became a fully developed woman. However, my abusers didn't seem to like my new feminine curves. If anything, it seemed to repulse them, and slowly but surely they stopped knocking at my door and climbing through my window. The constant ring of my mobile slowly petered off until it no longer buzzed with incoming text messages. Soon, I found myself all alone.

The bitter truth was that these men had only wanted me for my prepubescent body. Now I had developed into a woman, I was considered far too old to abuse and manipulate. No one had ever said this, because to do so would have been to admit that what they'd been doing had been wrong. Instead, I was slowly abandoned by each and every one of them.

Initially, I blamed myself. I had always viewed these men as my friends and I wondered what I had done to upset them. Bizarrely, I felt a certain kind of loyalty towards them because my abuse had been normalised for almost four years. However, the stark reality was that, at just eighteen years old, I had become too old.

CHAPTER TWENTY

GOING HOME

I had only lived in my new bedsit for four months when I realised it was time to go home.

I can't do this anymore. I need to stop fighting.

Of course, Mum and Dad were delighted – thrilled to have their 'little girl' home again, and although they had some idea of what had happened to me, they decided not to talk about it. It was almost like if we didn't mention it then it hadn't happened, but my 'secret' felt like the elephant in the room. In spite of this, everyone was extremely supportive. My father was the only one who treated me differently and would constantly call to check where I was and if I was okay. I knew it was only because he was concerned about me, but I didn't always know how to deal with it.

Back at home, I found that I struggled because I had no social skills. In many ways, I had almost been institutionalised by Shafina Ali. I didn't have the first clue how to speak to strangers and I didn't trust a soul. I was also unsure how to behave in public and would often swear and kick off when things didn't go my way. But my anger was a cover for all the fear I held inside – a fear that it might happen again. As a result, I found life challenging because it had changed and so had I. I was no longer the naive fifteen-year-old; that young girl had vanished and been replaced by an angry adult.

I moved back home at the beginning of October. By this time, my abuse had lasted four long years. In a bid to try to integrate me back into society, Mum had a word with her boss to see if she could get me a job at the supermarket where she and Dad worked. Again, I struggled because my defences were up. I struggled with the kindness of strangers because I always suspected an ulterior motive. However, with the endless patience, love and support of my parents and youth workers at Risky Business, slowly I began to trust again.

Somehow, I got the job and I worked long hours, stacking supermarket shelves. However, I struggled with responsibility because it was something I'd never had before. On a few occasions I purposely became involved in an argument so that I could storm off the shop floor. I couldn't accept rules and wanted to be in control at all times. So if my boss asked me to clean the floor, I would ask why she couldn't do it herself. I'd become angry and I would swear and kick off – all the mechanisms I'd used before. In short, I made myself unemployable because I had no skills, social or otherwise. Often, I'd turn up to work pissed or suffering with a rotten hangover. I spent the next two years like this, stumbling through life and building my own wall, just like Tim had done. Somehow, Mum managed to smooth things over with the boss and save my job on numerous occasions. In spite of my aggressive and volatile behaviour, my area manager – a lovely woman called Diane – was always extremely understanding. I'm not sure if Mum had told her the full story, but Diane knew I'd been involved in something awful because of all the time my folks had taken off. I decided that I needed to work to try to rid myself of my addictions. However, it was a long, slow process that left me with permanent anger issues.

Sometimes, even the simplest thing would set me off – a rude customer or just a colleague asking for help. One day, a workmate asked if I would help her unload a crate of dairy to stack in the fridges.

'You've got to be fucking joking me! That's not my job!' I shouted, pushing past her as I bolted for the door.

She hadn't asked me to do anything unreasonable. I was the unreasonable one.

One afternoon, another colleague asked about my plans for the weekend.

'Why do you want to know?' I replied, eyeing her with suspicion.

'Nothing. I just wondered.'

As a result of my struggle with alcohol, my concentration levels seemed to be all over the place. If I was stacking a shelf and a customer asked me to help them find something in store, I would walk away and forget where I'd been or what I'd been doing. I wasn't sure if it was withdrawal or the fact that I'd fried my brain. I was forgetful, uncooperative, socially awkward and moody – hardly employee of the month. However, the patience my work colleagues afforded me was astonishing.

I had already given up drugs, but I was still drinking heavily – up to a bottle of vodka on a bad day. It took a long time and endless support from Tina, Risky Business and my parents, but slowly I started to sort myself out. I knew I had to control it and reduce my drinking if I ever hoped to lead a normal life, so I did. And living a normal life helped enormously, because I didn't feel the need to drink heavily or take drugs just to fit in. For the first time, I had work – a purpose – and something to get up for every day. Once I'd stopped being angry at the world, my own world became less chaotic and more settled. Afterwards, I found that I actually enjoyed going into work and seeing my colleagues. The more relaxed I became, the more I seemed to let down my defences.

One Friday afternoon, a girl called Trisha, who worked alongside me in the supermarket, came to look for me.

'Hi, El, I just wondered what you were doing this weekend.'

I was loading the top shelf with tinned food, but I stopped and turned to look at her – a can still in my hand.

'Why?' I asked.

Trisha backed off, and for a moment I thought she might walk away and give up on me.

'Oh, it's just … well, there's a few of us planning to go out tomorrow night into town and I wondered … we wondered if you might want to come along.'

Trisha's question was so unexpected that I stood there for a moment, just staring at her.

'Me?' I asked, as though she had accidentally asked the wrong person.

'Yes!'

I couldn't believe it. I'd never had any friends at school – in fact, I'd been entirely friendless. It had been that loneliness that Shafina had pounced on. Shafina – I had not seen her since the day I'd left her flat. I didn't even know for sure if she still lived there anymore. But now there was someone willing to give me the chance to be part of something normal again.

'Are you sure …? I mean, yeah … I'd love to!' I added quickly.

Throughout my teenage years all I'd ever wanted was to belong – to a group or a gang – but I never had. Mistakenly, I'd felt I had belonged to the group of men, but they'd never been my friends. At last, here was my chance and I was determined to grab it with both hands.

Trisha was busy writing something down on the back of an old receipt.

'This is my address,' she said, handing it to me. 'We'll be leaving at about 8 p.m., and that –' she said, pointing to the bottom of the paper '– is my mobile number. Right, I'd better get back to work before they find me missing! I'll see you on Saturday.'

'Yeah, great! Thanks,' I said, clutching the receipt tightly in my hand. 'I'm really looking forward to it.'

The following day, for the first time in my life, I joined a group of girls my own age for a proper night out. Somehow, it felt completely alien that we could dress up and just be ourselves. We didn't have to have sex or even talk to men if we didn't want to. We were in charge of our own destiny, and it felt absolutely brilliant. My new-found freedom felt utterly intoxicating. Now, I was making my own decisions and living life on my own terms, and it felt amazing. After that night, I became part of the gang and I did all the things I'd missed out on before. Instead of being the outsider peering in, I was now at the centre of it all, enjoying the fun. For the first time, I loved my life. My new friends didn't know anything about my past. I didn't tell them because I felt ashamed and desperately wanted to fit in. As far as anyone was concerned, I'd just finished school and had landed a job at the supermarket. My life had gone from having no one to having a houseful of screaming, giggling girls, who would climb over each other to put on their make-up. When I eventually emerged from my bedroom all dressed up I could see it there in my parents' eyes – love and pride at how far I'd come. This made me feel good; it made me feel worthy.

Together with my new friends, I would go clubbing, out for meals, to the cinema or just browse around the shops. However, it didn't matter how much make-up I applied or how dressed up I was; the shame of what had happened was still there, buried deep beneath my designer gear and newly discovered confidence. I couldn't escape from it and sometimes, when I fell into a drink-fuelled slumber after a night on the town, I'd be right back there – inside Shafina's flat. To the outside world, I looked like any other girl my age, but in my nightmares the demons were screaming to escape.

Soon, our small gang had built up into a group of thirty. Me and my colleagues would hit the town after work – boys and girls. Unlike some of the others, I felt comfortable in male company because it was all I was used to. But I didn't have a boyfriend. In fact, the very idea of having one made me feel jittery. Instead, I shied away from men, especially those who were attracted to me. I hated blokes chatting me up, and if anyone tried, I'd be off like a shot.

One afternoon, I'd been asked to cover someone else's shift in the supermarket café. I was busy serving a customer behind the counter when a group of Pakistani men walked in. They carried themselves with the exact same arrogance as the men I'd been subjected to over the years. I recognised them.

'Er, sorry, love, but you've given me the wrong change. I gave you a ten-pound note, but you've given me the change for a fiver.' A woman's voice snapped me back into the moment as I stared at the frazzled young mum standing before me.

'Sorry?' I said, still distracted by the men. There were three in total, but one turned towards the counter and as soon as he spotted me standing there in my supermarket uniform, he began to sneer.

'I said, I gave you a tenner,' the young mum repeated. She was clearly exasperated.

'Oh, er, yes, sorry about that.'

My face flushed bright red as I checked the amount on the till.

She had her right palm outstretched to prove that I'd given her the incorrect change. My hands trembled and I became flustered as I tried to rectify my mistake. But my mind was a million miles away, still thinking about the men.

'I'm really sorry about that,' I apologised, placing a five-pound note in her hand.

I was shaking. The woman noticed and her voice softened.

'It's okay – we all make mistakes. Are you new here?' she asked, tucking the note inside her purse.

'Yeah, I mean, no … I usually work in the main part, but I'm covering for someone in here today.'

Although she was smiling at me, I wasn't looking at

her. Instead, I was staring over at the three men, who had sat down at a table and now all turned to look at me.

Get out of here. Run!

'Anyway, sorry again,' I added, trying to go.

I wanted her to move on so that I could escape.

Too late – they've seen you, the voice warned.

As the first man continued to stare, I realised I vaguely recognised him; I watched as he nudged the other two, and the group burst out laughing.

My pulse quickened and sweat prickled in the centre of my palms. I held them both flat against my apron and wiped them, but the fear was still there.

Get out! You need to get out of here!

My eyes darted back over to the men at the table. They browsed through the menu, discussing what they wanted to eat.

I checked around me, but my colleague was busy making up orders in the kitchen.

Christ, you're going to have to serve them!

My heart clattered inside my chest as I tried to remember to breathe. The walls of the café seemed to bend and then zoom in towards me.

Go! Just run. Do it now!

Blood pulsated and pounded behind my ears, causing my temples to throb.

I gulped as the first man stood up. He grinned as he made his way over towards me.

Go! Go!

A wide, sickly sneer moved across his face as he opened his mouth to speak.

'Hello, El, what are you doing here?'

My throat closed in on itself and I struggled to breathe.

'I ... I ...'

I couldn't do it – I had to get out of there. I had to escape.

A vision of him lying on top of me against the cold grass in Clifton Park flashed inside my brain. I could almost smell the damp earth and feel the short, spiky grass scratching against my back and my legs. His hands pawing at my body, his fingers slipping up inside my bra, snaking down into my knickers ...

Acid bile rose at the back of my throat, scorching it.

Go!

I turned and ran. I ran as fast as my legs would take me. I sprinted along the back of the counter and past the kitchen hatch as my stunned colleague looked on. I didn't stop and explain. What would I even say?

I'm sorry, but I don't want to serve this man because he and his friends raped me.

It was fight or flight, and I chose the latter.

My elbow caught against a wire basket that contained some small packets of biscuits. It clattered to the floor and the whole café turned to look at me – the mad girl behind the till. I bolted out of the café into the vast expanse of the supermarket floor. The strip lighting temporarily blinded me as my eyes scanned the store, trying to search for a safe hiding place.

Don't stay in the shop, he'll find you!

I raced past the ends of the aisles where I usually worked and I didn't stop. I tore past the checkout tills, my colleagues and the customer service counter. Everyone turned to look, but I couldn't stop or explain. I had to get out – I had to escape him, the men, my past.

My lungs burned as I sprinted past the security guard

standing by the door. He seemed confused – his eyes darted all around, thinking I was chasing a shoplifter. Still, I didn't stop. I carried on running until I was behind the back of the store, next to the loading bay. Pressing my back against the brick wall, I finally stopped and tried to catch my breath. But I was still on full alert, my eyes scanning the car park, searching for him and the others. As I gasped for air, I silently cursed myself.

You changed your mobile number, but it wasn't enough.

Why did I ever imagine working in a supermarket would be a good idea? I was on public show and I would always be accessible to them. I was just wondering what to do next when a hand grabbed the top of my arm. I screamed and turned, expecting to see the man.

'El!'

But it wasn't him, it was Diane, my area manager.

'Oh my God, Diane, it's you!' I gasped as I clasped a hand against my chest.

My heart pounded loudly beneath my fingers.

'What's up? What's the matter, El?'

I cast my eyes towards the ground because I couldn't tell her my 'dirty' little secret – I was too ashamed.

Diane refused to take no for an answer.

'Come on, El. Come with me. Let's go and sit down somewhere.'

I shook my head.

'No, no! I'm not going back in there, Diane. I can't. You don't understand … I … I …'

Tears sprang into the corners of my eyes until I couldn't stop them. Diane had witnessed me angry, but she'd never seen me like this before. Although she was a friend of the family, she'd never seen me this vulnerable.

'Come on, El,' she said, wrapping a kind arm around my shoulders.

Diane guided me towards a low wall at the side of the supermarket, far away from the front entrance.

'Listen,' she said, patting a hand against the wall as she gestured for me to sit down next to her. 'It's obvious something terrible has happened to you.'

'Oh, Diane, I can't …' I said, shaking my head.

'No, it's okay, I don't want to know. It's your business, El. Yours and your family's. It's nothing to do with me, but I do care. I care what happens to you when you are here at work, because I'm your boss, and I want you to be happy.'

I shook my head.

'It's not that I'm unhappy in the job, Diane,' I sniffed, wiping the tears from my face with my sleeve. 'I … well, I just don't think I can stay. I can't carry on working here. It's too public …'

Diane sighed.

'It's not you,' I insisted. 'It's me. I'm no good, you see. I'm damaged goods, Diane. You don't want me here, I promise. People know me … bad people, and I can't bring all that with me, not here.'

She refused to give up on me, even though I wanted to die; I felt utterly devastated, because just as I'd been getting my life back together, something else had come along to try to destroy it.

You'll spend the rest of your life like this – looking over your shoulder.

But Diane hadn't finished.

'Listen, whatever's happened, it doesn't matter. That is all in the past, but now you have a future. You have a future here, with me and with all the friends you've made. Whatever it is – this thing that happened to you – well, you need to move on from it, otherwise what are you going to do? You can't spend the rest of your life running, now can you? You've got to face up to it and move on. It's all any of us can do.'

I continued to sob as Diane spoke gently.

'But you don't understand, it's all my fault!' I sobbed.

'No!' Diane said, holding me by my shoulders. 'Whatever it was, it wasn't your fault. You were a child. Look at you, you're barely an adult as it is. Listen, I want you to promise me something, El.'

'What?'

'You must promise me that you will stop being angry and that you'll stop running away. Promise?'

I nodded.

'Yeah, I promise.'

'Good girl.'

Diane got up to her feet.

'Right, take a minute out and dry those tears. Then I want you to come and see me when you're ready. I'll not let anyone hurt you, do you understand?'

'Yes.'

'And if you don't feel comfortable in the café then I'll find you some work in the back of the store, okay?'

'Yes,' I whispered.

Diane smiled, turned and headed back towards the store. As she did, I called after her.

'Thanks, Diane. Thank you for everything.'

She waved her hand as though it had been nothing. Diane was fifty years old and a mother herself, so she genuinely cared. I wasn't sure if Mum had told her anything, but it didn't matter because Diane had been there when I'd needed her and, for that, I was and would always be grateful.

CHAPTER TWENTY-ONE

MOTHERHOOD

I'd never had so much money. I was eighteen years old and earning around a thousand pounds every month. With no outgoings or responsibilities, I was as rich as a king, and for the first time, I was free and in control of my own destiny. Of course, my abusers still haunted my nightmares, but finally I found a way to control my fear and, with the help of Tina at Risky Business, I was able to do what Diane had suggested – look forward, rather than dwell on the past.

My parents had refused to take a single penny from me, even though I still lived at home. They were so relieved to finally see me happy.

Thankfully, I never saw the men in the store ever again. My reaction must have scared them. Maybe they thought I'd gone to tell someone. Maybe they'd also fled the store that day, never to return. All I knew was that by the time I'd summoned up enough courage to walk back into the store, they'd vanished. I hoped they'd finally got the message that I wanted nothing more to do with them. I prayed that they would leave me alone to enjoy the rest of my life.

her, I believe she is still alive out there, because her death seems just too convenient.

I have written this book because I want people to be aware that women groom children too, not just men. If anything, Shafina Ali was even more calculating and evil than the rest of those men put together.

To this day, I do not know why South Yorkshire Police did not intervene when it knew I was a child trapped inside Ali's flat, especially having been told that she was grooming and exploiting young girls. I can only draw my own conclusion, which is that I believe that Shafina Ali was a police informant who passed on intelligence. Why else would the police help protect a woman who had been on its radar for years? It doesn't make sense.

As for the other men who raped me, the National Crime Agency is still investigating and, unlike my feelings towards the officers from South Yorkshire Police, I have nothing but the utmost faith in them.

I not only work in preventative measures; I campaign for the rights of victims too. I also work with children at risk, carrying out peer-on-peer work and one-to-one mentoring via Expert Through Experience workshops. I also sit on the survivors' panel for the Ministry of Justice.

I have met the Home Secretary, Priti Patel, twice – once in Rotherham and once at 10 Downing Street – to discuss my first-hand experience as a survivor of Rotherham's grooming gangs.

In 2016, I helped set up a project that trained businesses in Rotherham to spot the signs of CSE. The project – the first of its kind – was funded by the Police Crime Commissioner and was attended by firms such as Costa, KFC and McDonald's – all the places that vulnerable teens might congregate. I am also a public speaker, who helps to train professionals, such as police officers, solicitors, GPs and others who work with children in care, on how to spot the warning signs of CSE.

Separately, I have also visited the House of Commons five times alongside Labour MP Sarah Champion, using my own personal experience to try to effect a change in policy. In my spare time, I volunteer alongside youth workers, including whistle-blower Jayne Senior, my support worker Kathryn and others from the now-defunct Rotherham-based Risky Business youth project. Together, we help guide other survivors of CSE and provide them with both practical and emotional support.

Shafina Ali was an evil woman, who knew exactly what she was doing when she approached me – a schoolgirl – on the street that day. One of the social workers in the area had also raised concerns about Shafina Ali but was ignored, and ended up leaving her job and Rotherham because of it.

All I can say is it is thanks to Risky Business, its brilliant youth workers and my parents that I am still standing and have become the woman I am today. Together, these amazing people helped pull me back from the brink. Without them, I honestly do not believe I would be alive to tell you my story.

POSTSCRIPT

As I finish writing this book, I have just been told that my rapist, Asghar Bostan, has been moved to an open prison. As usual, I am the last person to know. Throughout this whole process I have felt as though I am the one doing the sentence, because the prison authorities have held Bostan's hand and protected his rights over mine. The blatant disregard for victims of CSE continues.

I would like to add that anyone, professional or otherwise, who comes into contact with a victim of CSE should endeavour to make that person feel worthy. They should also ensure that they are listened to and believed. If those in a position of power had done this decades ago, then perhaps they could have prevented this from happening to me and almost 1,500 other children.

We need to stop victim-blaming and dig deeper to try to help those who report CSE. We need to do this so that other children do not end up like me.

THE PROFESSIONAL

Jayne Senior MBE

Whistle-blower on Rotherham
Child Sexual Abuse Scandal

Risky Business youth project was set up in 1999 and initially it ran as one evening session. I began managing Risky Business in 1999. Back then it was a blank piece of paper; it had originally been set up just to work with girls and young women, because who would have thought this could happen to boys? But we started to work with boys from 2004 onwards. In total, we supported eighty to ninety boys out of 1,500 children. Risky Business wasn't set up because we had a problem with CSE in Rotherham; it was set up because we had a problem with 'girls involving themselves in prostitution' – which is how it was termed back then. Professionals working with these girls – many of whom were in care at that time – didn't know where to go or how to report their concerns, because at the time there was no legislation to protect the children. So, when they were picked up by the police on the streets, it was the children who were being charged as common prostitutes. No one seemed to be looking at how young these children were. It didn't matter that they were standing on street corners; they were still being raped by men who were pulling up in cars to do so.

This was how it started, but it wasn't very long before we recognised and began shouting from the rooftops that these were children being abused. They needed help and support, not to be criminalised. They were young children who deserved the same rights as other children: to go to school, make friends and be happy.

We became very successful, and this was based on the fact that we were youth workers. Even though others might not have seen us as 'professionals', the difference between youth work and social work, from a young person's perspective, was that they saw us because they had a choice to. They had no choice but to see their social worker. This meant they could try us out first, realise they liked us and continue to see us. We would then build up that trust, because, as youth workers, we walked alongside them, rather than trying to get one step in front or tell them how to live their lives. There was no judgement. Sometimes it felt as though we were on a hamster wheel; we might meet a young person, they might tell us to eff off and go away, but we never did, we just went back, and we kept on doing so. From there, we built trusting relationships, and it sounds strange to say it but some of it was built on equality, because we didn't see ourselves as being better than the child. We just wanted to be there for them. We didn't have a referral system like some other organisations, where they had to meet a threshold. Instead, we would have referrals from parents and professionals. Sometimes, even the girls themselves would refer their own friends to us. Vitally, we also went out and found these children ourselves. For example, if we were looking at three girls and a school raised a concern about another three girls who had been hanging around with them, we would go out and find all the girls. We didn't wait for someone to tell us that the girls were high risk, and we didn't wait for children to be raped; we tried to intervene early before it had even happened. We became a victim of our own success, as our numbers went up and up, but, shockingly, we saw the ages of the children being referred to us go down. No longer was it thirteen years and upwards, it was ten years and upwards.

Shafina Ali had been on our radar for a long time before Elizabeth came along. Shafina Ali's name went all the way back to a study we had done with the Home Office. We had some grant funding and were looking at how gangs were linked together. Shafina Ali played a very large part in this and was linked to some very key players. She had been on our radar since 2001/2002 – we were very aware of Ali and how dangerous she was.

We built up a bigger picture and we passed all of this intelligence on to South Yorkshire Police. We sat in on key-player and strategy meetings; we wrote reports, which we then filed as intelligence – never once did we not share this information, whether we could verify it or not. One of the things I always said in my role as manager of Risky Business was that we were not police officers, and it was not up to us to investigate information; it was up to us to hand it over and allow the police to investigate. So, because we had gathered this intelligence on Shafina Ali in 2001, South Yorkshire Police had it for almost three years before Ali targeted Elizabeth. Three years when SYP could have stopped her.

In Rotherham, it is a commonly held belief that the police didn't act over the girls because it was too much hassle. I suspect it was never the case, as the police claimed, that they didn't have the resources to put into it, but rather it was wrongly assumed that these girls had chosen this kind of lifestyle. There is no such thing as a child prostitute, but that's not how it was seen then. I think things are a bit better now, but I don't think they are perfect, and I don't believe we have come anywhere near as far as we should have. I think this is still happening today, and, as regards to Rotherham, you don't have two damning reports and then it all goes away – life doesn't work like that. I think we still do not reach out to our communities and give them any kind of training or skills to spot this type of abuse and report it. For example, we still have people in Rotherham who do not even understand what CSE is and how to spot the signs. Some professionals don't have a clue about a subject that should be a mantra on their lips.

When it came to Elizabeth's case, it was someone from the housing department of the council who had raised concerns with us. Elizabeth was already on our radar because we'd been in a strategy meeting where we had discussed a number of girls from the same school who were seen as high risk. We looked at who these girls were linked to and it transpired that Elizabeth had links to other girls and to Shafina Ali. Straight away a red button flashed. We decided to allocate her and a few other girls some youth workers who could work with them. However, before that actually happened, we received a phone call from the housing department, who had been at the same strategy meeting. A worker had been to a flat and had witnessed a young woman inside the property who was emaciated, and they were extremely concerned. As a result, we passed this information onto the police and Tina decided to go to Shafina Ali's flat, because we were asked by the council to do a safe-and-well check. However, when Tina pulled up outside, she received a phone call from the police (SYP), who told her that under no circumstances should she enter that flat because it was known to the police and had been identified as dangerous for anyone to enter – and yet there were children inside. The police expected her to just turn away and leave Elizabeth in there. The police saw these girls as compliant and making a lifestyle choice, when obviously they were not. It was simply breath-taking how these girls were viewed.

Tina didn't go to the flat that day because the police arrived and did their own safe-and-well check on Elizabeth, who answered the door and said she was fine, so the police officer [PC Barron] left her there. However, when we finally got Elizabeth out of there she was emaciated, she was covered in headlice, she was dirty. Tina, who had previously been a hairdresser, had to cut all Elizabeth's hair off because it was so matted that she couldn't get a comb through it, all while Elizabeth's parents watched and cried. You don't go into youth work to do that, do you? It was heart-breaking.

I still remember the names of each and every child we worked with. I don't know how, I just do, and I always will because every single one has burned a memory into my soul. But, as with Elizabeth, it's nice to see them succeed and to celebrate their successes with them. Over twelve years, we dealt with 1,447 cases – both boys and girls – but that figure doesn't include the thousands of children we worked with in schools, delivering our preventative programme.

There were a lot of truths that came out of Rotherham, but also a lot of myths. One of the things that came out was that these were 1,500 kids in care, whose parents didn't give a damn about them, but they weren't. We saw how broken the parents were throughout this and how it affected whole families. It's significant that these weren't all children in care – they were children and parents who reached out and asked for help. As one parent said to me, when you ring social services and then the police and they both turn their backs on you, where do you go?

I don't know why these children and their parents were ignored, all I do know is what I was told at the time – namely, that there wasn't any evidence – because they didn't go out and look for it – and, if you raise this as an issue, you'll be rocking a multicultural boat. But I look at this in a different way. I believe we've done our communities a massive disservice in Rotherham, because if we had gone into those communities fifteen or twenty years ago and said, 'We have got an issue,' just maybe – we'll never know, but maybe – we could have reduced the problem.

I don't know what we could have done that might have changed things, because we reported the problem to chief executives, head of children's services, head teachers and police officers at every single level. We wrote reports, we sat in meetings, but nothing was done, because somehow they saw it as 'victimless crime', as some of the children didn't even realise they were being exploited – they thought they were in healthy relationships, while others were too frightened to give statements. We gave them addresses – of houses, takeaway shops, taxis, parks – where this was happening. We knew where it was all going on, but the police didn't act on it.

Today, I think we've moved on, but make no mistake, this is still happening – and not just in Rotherham; it's happening all over. The NCA is going to be in Rotherham until at least 2025, mopping up what happened in the past over a twelve-year period. It's not even looking at what's happening now. This gives you an idea of the scale of the problem. But if they can find the evidence now, after all this time, to lock people up, then why couldn't it be found before?

I once sat in a strategy meeting where a very senior police officer said to me and the others sitting there that by reporting these men we were actually going against their human rights. The reason given was that we didn't have evidence that these men were raping children; we were listening to the children's side. I said: 'Excuse me, we are not police officers, we do not go out and investigate rapes, but we believe what these children tell us and we pass that information on to you as a statutory duty.' This came from a senior female police officer, but it didn't matter. It didn't stop us from doing it.

You don't see a happy whistle-blower because you have to stick your head above the parapet to call it out, and when it comes to something as massive as Rotherham – well, they came for me, with bells on. It's all about reputational damage, which is what they've tried to do – damage my reputation. People ask me, knowing what I know now, would I do it all again to protect these children? And I say to them, absolutely – I'd do it all again in a heartbeat.

THE PARENT

Jack Harper

Elizabeth's Father

One of the most shocking things about the scandal was not only the failure by those who were meant to protect our children, but also the scale of the cover-up. When the Rotherham sex abuse scandal first came out, the relevant authorities were desperate to cover their own backs, so they tried to excuse their lack of action with the claim that these children were in care. They were not. It was a lie. I later met other families whose children had also been caught up in CSE and they had not been in care either. But it's easier to blame the kids when these people didn't do their job properly. Instead, the police and Rotherham Council told the press that the fault lay with the children and their families. But Elizabeth hadn't been brought up in care, she'd been brought up in a loving family – a family desperate to get her back and bring her home; a family who couldn't do any of those things because our cries for help were ignored or blocked at every opportunity. South Yorkshire Police put me in handcuffs twice for trying to get my daughter back, so who were they trying to protect? Certainly not Elizabeth or me. If it hadn't been for Jayne and Tina at Risky Business, I honestly believe my daughter would not be alive today.

I reported SYP to the IOPC for lots of failings, including the time when a girl El knew told us she was living in a house with a thirty-nine-year-old man. She had been at Shafina Ali's and was still missing, but this girl had seen her inside this man's house and had told us he was raping El. I got his address and waited outside his house in the car for twenty hours but there was no movement. This worried me, so, fearing the worst, I went back home and rang the police, who went down to the address. Officers told me that they had spoken to El and this man and that there was nothing going on, but El doesn't even remember being there – that's how far things had gone. As a result, SYP left her there, even though I suspect Shafina Ali had pimped her out to him. The police refused to intervene, even though El was still classed as missing from home and was still a minor.

Shortly afterwards, someone rang the home phone to say they had seen El standing in a car park on the outskirts of Sheffield. We told the police and I got in my car to go and fetch her, but by the time I arrived she had already gone.

The worst time was when I was handcuffed twice by SYP and threatened with arrest three times in one day. El had been missing for ten weeks and we were sick with worry when a child protection officer (CPO) – the one who had seen and left her inside Ali's flat – suggested that I and my wife should do a TV appeal. The CPO, Yvonne (the woman from the local council) and another officer sat there and told us to expect the worst.

'Hang on, you know where she is – I've been telling you for weeks. In fact, I'm sick of effing telling you!'

I admit that I lost my temper, especially with the CPO. I called them all useless, but instead of helping me they threatened me with arrest. I was so angry that I threw them out of my house. I sat there for a short while, but I was absolutely fuming so I decided that if they wouldn't help then I'd go and get El out myself. I walked over to Shafina Ali's flat and started banging and kicking the door. I saw the curtains shift slightly, so I knew someone was inside. I continued banging on the door, but two police officers arrived. I explained about El being trapped inside the flat and that the CPO wouldn't help. One of the officers went off, but then he reappeared, told me I was under arrest, slapped some handcuffs on me and put me in the squad car. However, as we drove past my house, he stopped the car, removed the handcuffs and told me they were letting me go. He warned me that if I went back, I would be arrested. I returned home shaken and completely shocked. I couldn't understand how I was the criminal when that woman had my fifteen-year-old daughter inside her flat, where she was being raped by grown men. I sat at home for twenty minutes, but I was absolutely fuming. I couldn't work out why they were threatening to arrest me when all I wanted was my daughter home. I couldn't rest, so I got up and went back over to Ali's flat. I was just kicking and banging against the door when one of the neighbours upstairs hung out of the window and asked me what I was doing.

'My daughter is in there,' I told them. 'I just want to get her out and back home.'

The neighbour rolled their eyes, as though they'd heard it all before.

'We're fed up with it,' they told me. 'All through the night there are taxis coming and going with young girls in their nightdresses. We've reported it, but nothing ever gets done.'

I was so enraged that I kicked the door again, only this time I heard a crack and I knew I was almost in. Then five police officers came towards me. They handcuffed me again and I was thrown into the back of a police van and taken to Main Street station in Rotherham. We drove into a gated part, so I knew they were taking me to the cells. I couldn't believe it, because I had done nothing wrong – I was just a dad trying to get his daughter back. I was taken to the custody suite, but instead of being charged I was pulled by my shirt and put in a room with the door open. They left me there for twenty minutes, and then a copper told me to follow him. He took me past the custody sergeant, through what looked like the CID offices, and put me in the waiting area by the front desk. Eventually, he took me outside and told me that if I went back to Ali's flat then I would be arrested and charged with new stalking laws that had just come into effect and carried a heavy prison term. I was so panicked that I went home and just sat, wondering what to do. Then Tina arrived. She sat down and explained all about grooming gangs. It was only then that I had some under-standing of what El was going through. I stood up so that I could go back to the flat, but Tina warned me that if I did, anything could happen to El – she might even be killed. She said I should leave it to her and Risky Business, so I did and, thank God, they got my little girl out. The abuse didn't end with Shafina Ali, but if it hadn't been for them, I don't think El would be alive today. I cannot thank them enough for what they did for her and my family.

As for SYP, I wouldn't trust them to look after a pig. Their officers failed every child and every family. Many of those children have since died because of drugs; it was their only way of coping with what had happened to them. When El was missing, we rang the police so many times that our phone bill came to £560. The police later admitted that we'd called them 200 times, but the number was closer to 800.

One day, I was so at a loss about what to do that I phoned the police to speak to a senior officer. A man came on the phone and, when I asked what they were going to do to bring El back home, he told me that this sort of thing had been going on for over thirty years. He called it 'Paki shagging'. I was so shocked that you could have knocked me to the floor. I argued with him, saying that this was grown men raping children, but he refused to help, saying it would cause 'too much racial tension'. I rang back, but I never spoke to that same officer again.

As for Shafina Ali, like El, I don't believe she's dead, even though I've got a copy of her death certificate. There are too many inconsistencies. For example, her name was never on the flat lease and she wasn't listed as living at that address, which I thought was strange. It was as though she didn't exist. Years after what happened to El, I was told that the authorities didn't know where she was living, yet when she supposedly 'died' she was apparently found dead in the flat by council carers. It just doesn't add up. Also, it was strange how I was arrested so quickly when I turned up at her flat. I think Ali must have had a direct line to an officer – perhaps the one who regularly called her. I think she was put into police protection because she gave statements and evidence against some of these men in Rotherham. I believe she was a valuable police informant, and I think El and some of the other girls were collateral damage. Whatever Ali was doing, she must have been so important to the police that they turned a blind eye to the rape of young girls. Maybe she was an informant on suspected terrorist activity or other forms of crime, such as weapons or drugs. It is something we will never know. What I do know, however, is that Ali continued to live in that flat for five more years after we got El out. Often, I'd walk past her flat and see taxis pull up or parked outside. It made my blood boil, but I couldn't do anything because I knew I'd be the one who would end up in a police cell. Shafina Ali was confident that she was untouchable, and she was.

It was, without doubt, the worst time of our lives. When El was missing I felt as though my insides had been ripped out. I was in such a state that some days I didn't know where I was or what time of day it was. I had no other feelings, only anger. I spent so much time crying that I'm amazed my eyeballs didn't fall out of my head. I cried them both raw. I wasn't interested in anything; I just wanted to bring my daughter home. I blamed myself and felt like a failure, both as a husband and a father. I am a big bloke, so why couldn't I protect my little girl? I also felt a complete failure as a man. I was later diagnosed with PTSD and split personality disorder because of what has happened to my family. It destroyed our lives, and nothing has ever been the same since. I constantly tell El that she didn't do anything wrong and that she and the other girls are not to blame.

I took so much time off work when she was missing that I left my job, only to re-apply for it again once we'd got her back home. Then, four years later, I was standing outside work when I began to vomit and suffer crushing chest pains. I didn't realise it then, but I was having a heart attack. Someone called an ambulance and I actually died in the back of it before the paramedics saved my life. I recovered and returned to work, but then one day my arm and face suddenly grew numb, my eyes blurred and I felt dizzy. I was having a stroke. For my wife, this was the final straw. She had seen how all this had taken its toll on me and demanded I give up work, this time for good, and I haven't been back since.

Today, when I look in the mirror, I cannot stand the coward I see staring back at me. I hate him and everything about him, because I see him as a weak man. I blame myself for not being able to protect my daughter and I think I always will.

The only good thing to have come from all this is that my family, which has always been close, is now stronger than ever. As El's parents, we are in awe of her and all she has achieved. She is an incredible young woman and I feel proud to call her my daughter.

ACKNOWLEDGEMENTS

Thank you to my mum, dad and sister, for always being there through the darkness.

To Kathryn Kelwick, for being my guardian angel throughout my journey to justice.

To Sarah Champion MP, for playing a huge part in my journey from the Jay Report onwards. Thank you for all your help and support.

To Jayne Senior, for empowering me to go from being a victim to a survivor.

To Gemma, for being a part of my journey and always being there to support me. Thank you.

To PCSO Paul Newman MBE – thank you for your support and for all you have done throughout my journey.

To Swinton Lock, for the support I have received. Thank you so much.

To the National Crime Agency, for always believing me and getting me justice.

To Joe Casey, Estella Hawkey, Alison Holt and the *Panorama* team – thank you for helping me find answers and for all your support.

To Cllr Jill Thompson, for going on a journey alongside us and fighting for CSE and those future victims.

To Cllr Emily Barley, for going on a journey alongside us to fight for future victims, but also for all the things survivors need.

To Veronica Clark, for going on this journey and turning my life into a book. Thank you so much.

To Emily Vaughn, author of *Enslaved* – thank you for all your empowerment and support. This wouldn't have been possible without you.

Finally, thank you to all the people who have stuck with me throughout my journey. You all mean so much to me and your support has never wavered.